Lynn Newman has a gift of l̲ _ _

Natalie Goldberg,
author of *Writing Down the Bones*

Because Lynn knows her own creativity deep
from the inside, she is able to creatively inspire others
to explore and discover their freest selves.

Michele Cassou, author of *Life, Paint and Passion*

Part memoir and part workbook, *The Muse in You*
may be just what you need to heal from your pain and be
reborn as someone more passionate, purposeful, and alive.

Lori Deschene, author of *Tiny Buddha's Worry Journal* and others

There is no better guide than Lynn for helping you
befriend your inner muse. Lynn's priceless combination
of humor, vulnerability, and straight-up truth-telling
will inspire you to overcome life's challenges . . . a beacon of
hope, a fountain of wisdom, and a treasure of tools to call
out your inner creative strength and resiliency.

Heather Ash Amara, author of *Warrior Goddess Training*

Lynn Newman

the muse in you

Embracing CREATIVITY
to Overcome Life's Difficulties

REDFeather™

MIND | BODY | SPIRIT

Type set in Zurich/Mionion

ISBN: 978-0-7643-5717-6
Printed in China

Published by Red Feather Mind, Body, Spirit
An imprint of Schiffer Publishing, Ltd.
4880 Lower Valley Road
Atglen, PA 19310
Phone: (610) 593-1777; Fax: (610) 593-2002
E-mail: Info@schifferbooks.com
Web: www.redfeathermbs.com

For our complete selection of fine books on this and related subjects, please visit our website at www.schifferbooks.com. You may also write for a free catalog.

Schiffer Publishing's titles are available at special discounts for bulk purchases for sales promotions or premiums. Special editions, including personalized covers, corporate imprints, and excerpts, can be created in large quantities for special needs. For more information, contact the publisher.

We are always looking for people to write books on new and related subjects. If you have an idea for a book, please contact us at proposals@schifferbooks.com.

Contents

Introduction

Over a period of only a few years, my parents both died of cancer, I had four miscarriages, my husband and I divorced after seven years of marriage, and my dog, Lita, of sixteen years, died too. It was intensely difficult for me, and I fell apart, closing the blinds and holing up in my home for months, suffering from anxiety and depression. I hardly recognized myself. At the same time, even in my darkest hours, I knew in my heart I would somehow get through.

In the midst of these midlife crises, wondering when I would get over the debilitating, soul-crushing loss, I drew upon the creativity principles and practices I had learned and taught for over twenty years to connect to something greater and overcome.

A few months after all of the losses, I made a new friend whose father had recently passed away. I invited him over for a bowl of my famous Italian chicken sausage lentil soup at my home in Los Angeles. He was angry and confused. He was in shock. I picked up his soup bowl in the palms of my hands and said to him, "Grief is a big bowl to hold." I know. I was speaking for myself.

At any given time, without knowing how or why, grief can overcome us in a number of ways. We can get super pissed off. Or want to hide. Or push away those we love and wall off. We can try to numb the pain. Suppress feelings. Seemingly insignificant events might trigger us. A memory or random happenstance might well us up. We all mourn differently, wanting more than anything for it all to end. And sometimes pretend that it's over when it is not.

I was told once that there was grief and *frozen grief*. *Frozen grief* can stop both personal growth and future healthy bonding. For some people, depression and emptiness can become so debilitating that they get stuck in the grieving process and have trouble letting go, a process that is akin to water passing from a solid state to a liquid, a cohesion of molecules holding together and resisting separation. Warmth and equilibrium are what's needed to heal. But there's not a single temperature that can be considered to be the melting point of water.

In 2004, I received my master's in counseling psychology in Los Angeles at the same time I met my husband, Shlomi. I was thirty-four. He was thirty-two. I worked as an intern in a clinic, counseling individuals, couples, families, and youth groups. It felt good to be of service, but I was passionate about the creative process and the creativity principles I'd studied as an actress, writer, and painter. Soon after, I opened up a private practice working mostly with creatives in the entertainment business. My goal then became to help everyone, not just creatives, become the artists of their own lives.

Ultimately, I believe everything we do is creative. The way we think. The way we problem solve. The way we make the most of our lives. How we become stronger, healthier, more alive and free is creative. How we start, continue, and complete a successful project and manifest our dreams is creative. How we parent, work, and handle our relationships is creative. Whenever we look for how we can resolve a situation creatively, we empower ourselves.

I learned while getting my master's in counseling psychology that after suffering a great loss, it can take two years to heal, or at least have a sense that the trauma is then in the past, even if it's not "over." After the death of my parents and dog, facing my infertility, and my divorce, I closed my practice in order to focus on my own healing. Two years after that, I was stronger for sure, but I still felt utterly lost and purposeless. I didn't want to return to counseling but wasn't sure what I would do next. I worried; then I was frozen, stuck in a frozen state of grief.

I desperately wanted to move on, for my new life to begin, one of happiness and success. But creating deep-lasting inner change was going to take time. As much as I wanted to be over my pain, I couldn't force it to go away. I was going to have to access those deep places inside myself to update them to a new way of being. But getting in touch with your better self doesn't always happen overnight. For me, it ended up taking four years.

To truly make profound, lasting change, it takes determination, practice, and, sometimes, outside help. My work during that time was to learn how to have a deep, intimate relationship with self-love. To let go, accept, and heal, I had to meet myself exactly where I was and face my darkness. Slowly, step by step, I faced my disquiet and uneasiness and then came to the realization that I had become so accustomed to my new life, I was shocked to realize I had created an even better life for myself than I could ever imagine.

In the grand scheme of things, I can look back now and see all that I'd learned and how much I'd grown. In allowing myself to be broken, I became whole. It was quite miraculous, really. In my most-broken, hideous moments, the most magical thing happened. I came to love my big, beautiful, messy self. I came to accept her like nothing else.

I missed my mother and father, the husband I loved, the babies I didn't have, and the dog that had replaced them, only for me to lose her too. But I came to care for myself like my own parent, my own spouse, and my own child. I was all I had left. And if that was it, then I was going to love her. Loving myself meant allowing myself to be as messed up as I was, to not apologize a hundred times for every one of my mistakes, or kill myself over them; to humbly say to others and myself, *This is it*. And then, as I tried to take a kinder approach to myself, I began to accept and love others like myself. They got to be messes too. And my heart opened. And I found boundless joy and happiness.

Nothing's harder or more painful than having to face loss and adversity. We can experience many confusing stages that make us question everything. Negative emotions can take over and cripple us when our relationships bring challenges, or we endure the loss of health, a home, a job, or loved one, or when we wish for just once that when things started to get good, they would stay that way. Yet, tough times are really offerings to show us what no longer serves us. Once they've passed, they no longer have power over us.

No one, including myself, wants to feel pain. When suffering from depression, I became accustomed to the lethargic haze, heavy-laden legs, and foggy head that made other people's words waft way above me. My heart used to pound from anxiety that sometimes made me feel so vulnerable I feared leaving home. The day I overcame that anxiety was when I finally stopped trying to force myself to be different than I was. I came to the realization that there was no problem with me, and being human truly was enough.

These are some questions that helped me that I hope help you. What if:

- There was nothing you *had* to do, change, or fix?
- You didn't have to be different than you are?
- You could love and accept your big, beautiful self?

I was taught while getting my counseling-psychology degree with an emphasis on spirituality: *We're all spiritual beings having a human experience.* For decades, I focused on the spiritual part, but what about just being human? We want to believe a life-changing transformation will come upon us, and one day, like magic, we'll wake up and all of our issues will have vanished. I was looking for something outside me to save me, to rescue me, and most importantly, to change me, rather than just let myself be all that I was. Without the pressure, grasping, and need to fill what I thought I was lacking, I could feel at home with myself and find peace. I could have more acceptance and compassion for what arose in me. And rather than fix it, to try to change it, I allowed it to be present. I didn't have *to do* anything. I was free.

- Could you still better yourself without any pressure?
- Could you focus not only on accomplishing, but just being and learning?
- Could you be more than okay just the way you are in all your messy glory?
- How would this feel?
- What would you do differently?

The purpose of this book, with its personal stories, worksheets, quick exercises, meditations, and the inspired questions it asks, is to offer you the support you need during the tough times. We can sometimes forget the awake, creative beings we truly are. This is a loving reminder.

In the coming chapters, we will address these questions:

- How do we transcend our circumstances to find lasting peace and happiness?
- How do we unlock the chains of the mind and become free again?
- How do we exist in joy, certainty, and radiance?
- How do we invite more adventure into our lives, free our passions, start and complete projects, or simply have less stress and more ease?
- How do we discover our life purposes and move quickly toward our desired destination?
- How do we have a deeply intimate, loving, healthy relationship?
- How do we create more of what we want to reach our dreams?

There are answers to these questions, and they might not be what you think they'd be. It's not the answers we're striving to seek. It's the questions. You'll see.

Questions

> I want to beg you, as much as I can, to be patient toward all that is unresolved in your heart and to try to love the questions themselves like locked books that are written in a very foreign tongue. Do not seek the answers, which cannot be given you because you would not be able to live them. And the point is, to live everything. Live the questions now. Perhaps you will then gradually, without noticing it, live along some distant day into the answer. Resolve to be always beginning—to be a beginner!

—Rainer Maria Rilke
On Love and Other Difficulties

Let's go on this life journey together as beginners.

To create our happiness, dream life, dream work, and dream relationships, we need to move from the inside out. Meeting what's inside first and doing so with sustained attention makes us feel vibrant, content, and lucid. Only after we focus on what's within can we connect with openness and feel love for everything outside us—our partners, family, friends, community, daily work, and life purpose. Then, we can make contact with our dreams and create them in a way that's vivid and rich. When connected to our true creative essence, we inhabit the moment from there, and our dreams come to life.

There are cycles in all of our lives. We experience greatness, tributes, celebrations, wins, moments of bliss, perfect vacations, falling in love, good solid days, and enjoying the extraordinary and the ordinary that life offers. And, of course, not all of life is made up of these high moments. Ultimately, they pass and we find ourselves with difficult, sometimes painful, desperate times. We question everything—*Who am I? Where am I? How did I get here? And what do I do next?*

We have periods of grieving for our memories, a loss, or an ending. The cycle of our life may be turning and we may feel like we're hanging in the gap of the unknown. Our anxiety may be telling us a false story about how our future is predetermined. We may fear that what we want will never come.

When you ask yourself the questions offered in these pages, what you are currently doing may no longer feel right. You may crave change but don't know exactly what you want or how to achieve it. Though you might believe yourself to be talented, courageous, smart, and wise, you can still be unsure of what your next steps are and what you're truly capable of. Even though you know from experience that every morning the sun will rise, you may wonder how much it will shine down on you in your own life.

After I lost my parents, my pregnancies, my husband, and my dog, it was hard to admit that at forty-two years old, I suddenly found pieces of myself that I had constructed after decades of committed inner growth, spiritual work, and therapy scatter far away from where I found myself. I questioned everything and worried I would never find the answers. But looking back now, it served an important purpose in my life. I had to completely break down into my emotional fragility to break through completely.

As beginners on this journey, we have the power to shift perspectives: to find opportunities, initiate our own freedom, step back into joy after a dark cloud passes, and discover a new sense of self even after it seemed lost forever. This doesn't always happen in big, grand revelations. Often it is in simple, sustaining, or connected moments. The opportunity is to come to know who you truly are right now. It's in the *now* where we contact our inner compass, because what we want to create is *already here*, ready and waiting for us.

- Could you relax and lean into the moment?
- Could you create whatever you wanted along with fear if it's present?
- What if you didn't worry about mistakes as you go about it?
- What if you couldn't go wrong? Or make the wrong choices?
- What if you couldn't go backward, only forward in the doing of it?
- What if you were interested in breaking all the rules and letting go of any expectations?

Asking yourself open-ended questions helps you to meet the present. The questions presented will shift you out of one reality and into a whole other dimension. They give you the tools to make a change that bypasses self-judgment. In each chapter, I will ask open-ended questions to invoke imagination, inventiveness, and inquiry. They enable you to hold on to that sort of "beginner's mind" that frees you to begin anew.

In searching for my own ways out of the dark, I learned that all I had to do is ask myself questions like these and feel them deeply—not try to answer them necessarily—but to allow the answers to appear on their own, in their own time, no matter how frustrated or stuck I may have felt. It was easier than I thought most of the time, but not always, especially when I wanted to hold on to what was familiar to me. But when asking open-ended questions, true insight downloaded into my consciousness. I was on my knees, astonished as to what opened up inside me.

Together we will ask open-ended questions to ponder, not with our minds but with our hearts, where true answers lie. Whenever you feel blocked, you can ask these questions of yourself. Once internalized, the questions arise innately, freeing you from perceived limitations, fear, or rigidity. Whether you're unsure of a next new project, resisting continuing a journey, or avoiding finishing a task, or whether you're overwhelmed by what you've already taken on and committed to—no matter what stage you're in, either the beginning, the middle, or the end, the questions help you to meet exactly where you are right now.

What if:

- You felt all of what you feel without having to make sense of it? Or knew what it meant?

- You delighted in the uncertainty?

- You expected the unexpected?

- You held yourself gently with kindness and tenderness?

If you're feeling grief, low, stuck, anxious, or burnt out and want to return to living, if you want to connect to something greater and develop a deeper relationship with yourself, or if you want to find inspiration and support while going through a life transition—these questions and tools I offer will support you to creatively make yourself anew.

When I was in transition, unsure of where I was, who I was, and where I was going; when I was unhappy in my career direction or frustrated I didn't have my dream life, and uncertain of what to do next; when I wanted to cower and hide or wanted to have it easier, holding it with a lighter hand to enjoy the ride; or when I was angry, afraid, or sad, I used these questions and tools to allow painful emotions to empty and be gently released. When I felt alone, brokenhearted, or isolated—these questions and tools created heartfelt connection within, and ultimately my greatest happiness.

For a while when my life fell apart, I looked for simple things that gave me pleasure to try to ground me. I knitted three sweaters, two scarves, a winter hat, and a sweater coat. At times it was hard to eat, but damn if I didn't look good in those retail-therapy jeans. I read *People* magazine. Watched chick flicks. Meditated. I painted and wrote in my journal a lot—anything that called me to keep connecting to something. I came to learn that grief pressures you to go within. I told my friends, "Bad day. Can't talk. That's all."

I couldn't force my circumstances to be different, even though I wanted them to be. All I could do was to try to be brave, to never stop questioning, and to meet whatever arose for me in the present, even when I wished I didn't have to feel the majority of it. I couldn't get away from what I was feeling, no matter how much I tried. I waited for the answers to tell me what I was supposed to do with the rest of my life. It's in the emptiness where the answers came. When I was ready for them, they arose from a deep inner sense of intuition and wisdom. But they took time to rise up and strike, and then my whole world and sense of self changed in front of me.

For certain, when not knowing what to do next, if you are open to the questions, you'll eventually be shown a step. The next question then becomes, Will you listen to your answers? And after taking that step, another opportunity to question will unfold, leading you toward another next step. If you continue to listen to what arises in you, you will most likely find yourself moving in the flow where things really start to creatively connect, and you can generate joyous momentum.

Life brings us multilayered dimensions so that we can come closer to knowing our true selves without the lies and distortions. Once we have reached one level, there's always another to discover. Being willing to go on a deep inner exploration snaps us out of the limited mind and offers space for new light to enter.

We're not searching for the certain "right" answer, but opening ourselves to expansion and allowing ourselves to coexist with our creative natures. Too often our mind tries to trap us into trying to find "right" answers so that we can convince ourselves we have certainty, as if we have our whole life all mapped out. We can feel anxious if we don't know, aren't sure, have too much to handle, or don't have what we need to make educated decisions. On the flip side, the search for answers can box us in, trapping us in the analysis of meaning rather than allowing and exploring. Ultimately, the more we know, the more we realize the less we know, and that's our greatest empowerment. It's in the space of open-ended unknowing where our insight lies.

What if:

- You could step into the mystery of your life?
- You could trust in nature's organic unfolding?
- You didn't have to know what you were doing or how it will end?
- You were curious about what calls you, even if seemingly irrelevant?
- You weren't afraid to fail, mess up, or ruin anything?

True wisdom comes from a place of awareness, not intellect. When we have an insight or an "aha moment," it's not always easy to define or label it, and many times it's difficult to even find words to tell someone about our experience. It's these moments that we're going for here, the kinds of experiences we cannot translate. It's more like, *Hey, that's cool what just happened. I feel great! Something big just took effect and I feel changed, but I can't really explain it.* The point is to arouse curiosity. We can do that by asking compelling questions that spark the unusual, new, or fascinating and captivate our interest so we keep stepping toward an unrestricted sense of freedom. The trick is not to "effort" an answer. It's about "living the questions" in hope that you'll receive an insight you couldn't otherwise encounter. Once you receive that insight, you are off and running, free of the block you were once in and creating more of what you want in your dream life, work, and relationships.

It took me four years to grieve my losses, but I was ready then to step up and shine in my new life. As I went deeper into the questions, my heart exploded open. I came closer to the truth of myself. I was no longer afraid of uncertainty or to be seen in my bared vulnerability. My hardened, defended shell of anger, blame, fear, shame, and self-doubt softened, and I became gentler, kinder, and more compassionate—all because my humanness humbled me.

Usually, when a true insight enters into our consciousness, it's because something popped open for us, and we're in awe of the newfound awareness. The reason for this is that we've come into contact with something fresh, something new that may have never dawned on us. This is where the fun stuff starts happening, where the fragments come back in and our pieces gather together to become whole. It might not be able to be explained by our rational mind, but we feel it, and it makes all the difference. When we operate in a realm where our mind can't comprehend, our heart blows open into infinite possibilities. When we're able to meet our insides deeply and genuinely, we can break through into unlimitedness. We know we're in tune because it feels pretty damn awesome. This is creativity in its true form. Connecting to our true essence enlivens us.

Judgment

> *There is nothing either good or bad, but thinking makes it so.*

—William Shakespeare

I used to think I was defective. It stemmed from me buying into the belief that I couldn't fit in and never belonged, always searching for home because I was adopted at birth. My parents wanted a baby girl so much—they ordered me special delivery. As family lore had it, the lawyer walked with me from St. John's Hospital to the nearby temple in Tulsa, Oklahoma, for my naming.

He placed me in my mother's arms as Dad stood next to her proudly. My two brothers, ten and eleven years older than me, were elated about their new sister. I was a completion to the family. None of them saw me as different, though at times I wished they'd acknowledged that I was.

"More than anything, I wanted a little girl," my mother told me. "I wanted you so much. It wasn't because I couldn't give birth, because I could. I wanted to adopt. More than anything in the world, I wanted someone special as a child—extra special." She always told me this, even though at times, as I grew up, I kept her at a distance, even as she looked at me with despair. She never knew what to do with my emotions. I expressed myself so differently.

Mom said I wasn't like my brothers, whom she understood innately. Marty and Russ came from my mother. She intuited what they needed before they used words. But she said she never knew how to help me. Instead, she threw her hands up into the air.

Mom was freckled, with red, curly hair that she straightened like Jacqueline Onassis in the seventies every week at the salon, only to give it up when she hit forty, deciding to cut it short, tight curls locked against her head. I had the same coloring as my father and brothers: dark hair, dark eyes, and prominent noses. It always surprised those who knew our family when I blurted out that I was adopted. Mom would be embarrassed at my need to acknowledge this. I felt like an outsider at times and publicly struggled from not knowing where I came from.

When I was growing up, my family treated me as if I wasn't adopted, but still my mind found a way to convince me that I was separate. My adoption wasn't kept a secret. I was told as early as I could remember. But I carried the story for many years that I'd always be abandoned rather than loved and accepted. Almost every adult intimate relationship I had was negatively impacted by those beliefs, either by manifesting unavailable men who would indeed abandon me or I'd sabotage the intimacy that developed. When I felt rejected by a man, my reactions were larger than necessary. Based on this false story, I thought it meant something about me, that I wasn't good enough, lovable, or worthy.

When I was in my mid-twenties, eight years before I got my master's in counseling psychology, an unhealthy relationship sent me packing from Los Angeles off to Santa Fe, New Mexico, to find myself. In a New Age kind of town, I met many powerful healers, gurus, shamans, and teachers. I became a creative-writing and painting-workshop junkie. I studied with leading bestselling self-help authors and spiritual teachers and collected tons of healing modalities on the search to find the "Completely-Cured-Happy Lynn."

I went on Shamanic Toltec power journeys to spiritual centers around the world, such as Machu Picchu, Teotihuacan, and the Egyptian pyramids, chanted with Indian gurus, and became a certified yoga instructor and Reiki master. I got Rolfed to manipulate my body's tissues to release stress patterns, did more intense bodywork with thick-boned Maoris, and rebirthed with conscious breath work. I studied parapsychology, quantum dynamics, past-life regression; memorized mantras; unraveled koans; and collected crystals and Tarot cards. I went on vision quests in the desert, called leading psychics, mapped my astrological chart, figured out my Enneagram number to diagnose my personality type, and dreamed lucidly for nights in an upright chair. I had acupuncture weekly, drank herbal tinctures and elixirs, bought every kind of healing essential oil, collected a library of self-help books, and did loads of homework with several life coaches.

I know. It's insane.

In my early adult years, I was a perpetual seeker. Because of an innate sense that there was something wrong with me, and a belief that I was "unwanted" at birth, I constantly looked outside myself to find respite, feel loved, and know my worth.

Even though the relationship, which kicked off my self-improvement mania, was dysfunctional, that man gave me a gift that I wouldn't discover for years to come.

"What's not to love about you?" he always said.

That would have saved me, if only I could have really heard it and made it my own. If I had only for one minute stopped and realized this truth, I would have found my peace—and not from a man, or self-help book, or seminar. I'd be freed from a need to find something outside me. I would have come to know my own heart.

There was nothing wrong with my intention to heal. Nothing wrong with all the many modalities I studied. What was wrong is how I held on to them for dear life, along with the conditioned belief for why I needed them. In the judgment that I wasn't enough, I perpetuated my problems. I was searching and seeking for the one magic thing outside me that could heal the lie I lived by: that, deep down, I was broken.

We have opportunities in life to let go of what we think we know about our beliefs. Nothing is set in stone. We have opportunity to remember that our inherent creative nature is one of fluidity.

Yes, there is inner work to be done. Growth, change, self-awareness, and healing are all crucial. So many people avoid doing the inner work that is necessary. Avoidance will always keep us in the same old, same old. But the mechanism that drives us to fix, perfect, and change is, in its own way, another unconscious way we can get trapped, by holding on to the belief that there is something we need *to do* to become a better person. This mechanism drives us to look outside ourselves, to avoid having to accept ourselves as enough, who we are right now, in this moment as worthy and good.

What if:

- All that you need is already here?
- It already exists inside you?
- It could be bigger than what your limited perception can understand at this moment?
- You didn't have to force it?
- You dropped the intense effort to seek it out, find it, discover it . . . Could it possibly reveal itself on its own?
- Whatever lives and breathes inside you is already beating loudly?

It took me decades and many unfortunate, painful breakups to stop reacting from this early wound to realize the story wasn't true. It was a lie my inner beliefs were telling me.

When I learned to identify and then drop the story attached to my deep feeling of abandonment, I slowly stopped buying into all the negative thoughts of what it meant about me as an adoptee. It was uncanny how much it ran me without my even realizing it.

In the end, I went from being helpless to helping myself. I stopped distrusting my capability to use my own inner resources. Looking back, the pieces of the puzzle that made up my life's path all came together, converging without additional effort at the moment they were ready to.

So, I'm curious. Is there a lie from your past destroying your present? Are you carrying a story that, if identified and dropped, your suffering could vanish?

WORKSHEET
Rewriting Your Story

1. **Think of an issue you are having in your life right now.** Identify a belief you are carrying about yourself, someone else, or a group of people in regard to this issue that is causing you difficulty or suffering.

2. **Answer the following questions:**

   - How did this belief system fit the time and place from when it occurred, and does it still serve me in present time?

   - Where did I learn this negative belief and pick it up for myself?

   - When did I agree to carry this story?

   - Were these belief systems handed down to me from either of my parents?

   - Is it possible they learned it from one of their parents?

3. **After exploring these questions, make a commitment to release the agreement that you made to carry this belief.** Below, in the first blank, fill in the negative belief system you are working with, and in the second blank replace the belief with a more uplifting, supportive point of view.

I release and let go of all agreements, pacts, contracts, ties, attachments, and implants created by the belief system that _____ _____, and I choose to replace it with a more uplifting, supportive view of_____ _____now.

4. **Go within and take a moment to center.** Speak this statement out loud with your full intention. Focus on the light and expansion you may feel in your heart as you do this process and fully intend its release.

5. **If you have more than one belief you would like to update, state each one separately in this way.** It's wild how beliefs we picked up from childhood can secretly control us later in our lives without us knowing it from deep within our unconscious. Once you see it and reframe it, you will be set free!

· ·

I have often felt that every relationship I have ever had, whether familial, platonic, or romantic—every single person who entered into my life—brought with them a fragment of myself that I had lost or given away at some time in my past. Each person who entered into my life brought with them this chance, holding it in the palm of their open hand as a gift for me to reclaim—even those relationships that were the most painful, perhaps those of betrayal or abandonment, brought a fragment of me with them.

The mistake was when I believed that something was lost when my relationships ended or I experienced a death of a loved one: that the heart cannot be repaired, or that the love received could never be replaced, or even worse that I was empty without them. Each person magnificently came to show me a part of myself that I had not known, could not know until I came to know that person. The relationships may have resonated with something familiar, a similar pattern I continued to create as I moved through time and space. Yet, every relationship helped me go deeper, helped me to know myself. With each connection, if I was willing, I saw more, I understood more, I became more aware. I reached the depths of myself, layer after layer, coming closer to the core, so that I could heal, so that I could grow, so that I could learn to love others and myself better.

Our connection to love lies in the fullest expression of our hearts. But we can sometimes believe that the heart is the scariest place because that's where our vulnerability lies—the soft, tender, fragile, and sensitive parts of us. We can even judge how we aren't capable of loving others and ourselves well. Our inner judge says: *If only you were less in your head. If only you could love more. If only you could be free and in your heart. . . .*The duality always exists between the head and the heart! We feed judgment unknowingly, with the intention of doing "good" and "being loving," wondering why we still aren't happy.

There is only one reason that our pieces can scatter, the only one thing that can make us stuck and feel trapped. What steals our light is our judgment of others and ourselves. Judgment is a thief that robs us of our creative energy. Rather than break through and remarkably overcome, judgment crashes down the bricks that built our foundation. It keeps us from self-acceptance and self-love. When we judge ourselves we deny the truth of who we are: unique and extraordinary beings who have a lot to offer and a lot to give, with inherent special talents and wild desires to experience what personally inspires us.

Too often, we can be hard on ourselves. Our opportunity is to learn how to treat ourselves gently and with tenderness. When we were kids, if we did something bad or wrong, we were punished. Or our church/temple/mosque made us believe that God would punish us. So we grew up thinking that the only way to get the lesson was to chastise ourselves. We thought that *If I beat myself up over and over again, I might get it.* This way of thinking only makes issues worsen. Self-abasement creates guilt, regret, and shame. We harm our hearts and the hearts of others. We hide or cower. Our self-esteem lowers.

How we get free of self-judgment is to remember and forgive our humanness. The very fact we're on this Earth means that we're lovable and enough just as we are. Our opportunity as humankind is to recondition how we learn, to see every act, no matter how bad or wrong, as an opportunity to be exactly that—*human* and *kind*—more compassionate, loving, and accepting of ourselves. The result is more kindness, compassion, and acceptance for and from others.

Funny, this whole way of thinking goes against how we were brought up to think. We thought we should be hard on ourselves to learn. We thought we needed to get it in gear and push forward. We thought we needed to drive the nail in more. But if we attempt to create change with a heavy hand that carries a hammer, mallet, or bludgeon, we set ourselves up for more suffering. When we judge, it cuts us off from the love we seek because what we judge in ourselves we also judge unknowingly in others. We project judgments onto those we love the most and those we meet, even strangers, unaware of how we're limiting ourselves. When we lack love and acceptance, we can push opportunities for genuine connectedness away. Whether others are aware we are judging them or not, they feel it, and they shut off. And when we judge ourselves, whether we're aware of it or not, we feel it and shut off from others.

The beast of judgment took many forms for me. I compared myself to others, judging myself as "not enough" or "more than," which is the same thing. I could hide yet still craved being seen and recognized. I could try to rescue others to the extent of taking on another's problem and disempowering them and myself, or work overly hard to accomplish something worthwhile to the extent of weakening my well-being, all out of the need to prove my worthiness.

Trying to be the best I could be, I competed with myself. *You didn't run fast enough today on your morning run. You didn't meet your personal record.*

We try to follow the rules in order to be more, taking on more stress. We want to achieve and achieve, grasping too tightly on to money, power, prestige, and the objects we own to define us. We want to raise our kids to be perfect, and they feel more pressure than ever before. We want perfect bodies and listen to how society tells us how we should look and act. We set unattainable goals rather than create action plans that are more realistic and attainable. Our lives feel unmanageable, and we've lost the importance of focusing on gratitude for what we have, which stems from having more acceptance.

Our inner judge puts unfair expectations on us to save us from bad things happening. The only way around this is to embrace our humanness. Perhaps then, we can relax. The bottom line is if we set up realistic standards and drop the unworkable expectations we place on ourselves, we find we have everything we need to deal with whatever arises when and if necessary. We can love others and ourselves better by offering more space to grow.

But judgment isn't totally wrong. It exists for a reason. It helps us to motivate and strive for more of what we're capable of. It helps to make ethical calls and assists in making choices. Judgment keeps us on our toes, so that we might not fall and hurt ourselves. It serves a purpose *to a point*. But there's a middle way. We can produce, create, be determined, and succeed, while using judgment in another way than we've learned previously.

The root of judgment is fear. We judge because we're afraid. Though it's ultimately there to protect us from being harmed or hurt, judgment operates in duality. Our mind decides if we're good or bad, enough or not enough, lovable or not lovable, honest or corrupt, right or wrong. It tells us lies, like either we're broken and unfixable or better than someone else.

Judgment keeps us fragmented, breaking our spirit apart. It creates wedges in our hearts. Our nervous systems can break down. Our physical and emotional health can suffer all in the attempt of trying to gain some control over the chaos that listening to our inner judge causes. We forget that we're already whole as we search for how to put the illusion of our pieces back together.

The *in-between* is where we find our freedom—the space that allows for anything and all to occur. Like a trapeze artist, we let go of one bar and while reaching for the next, discovering that it's in that gap where all creativity is born. It's in that empty space where we open up, let go, and touch the nonverbal, unbounded possibilities available to us. We transcend when we find grace with permission to just *be*. Fear subsides here. We no longer have the need for protection because we're divinely flying through the air.

A Journal Exercise to Overcome Your Inner Judge

1. **Thought download:** In the morning, before you start your day, write in your journal for ten minutes your present thoughts, feelings, and experiences. Keep your hand moving as you allow your inner judge a voice to express itself rather than hiding in your unconscious. Be brutally honest. It doesn't matter if what you write is stupid, whiney, or full of blame. Put it all out there in the spirit of inquiry, ready to play detective with your mind's inner workings. Give yourself full permission to write anything and everything that's going on in your mind.

2. **Observe your thoughts as you write:** Behind every feeling is a thought that you have. Those thoughts are driving you unconsciously. If you feel low, bad, angry, or exhausted, there is a thought behind that feeling. If you're feeling happy, enthusiastic, joyful, or at peace, there is a thought behind those too. As much as you can, be aware of what your mind is thinking as you write.

3. **Now write in the positive:** For another ten minutes, reframe everything you wrote in the positive. Turn it around in your mind before you write it down, while keeping your hand moving. You may sometimes feel as though what you are going to write doesn't seem true, but write it anyway. And, as you continue to write, start believing it as truth. Allow yourself to experience your thoughts with lightness, joy, and gratitude.

4. **Practice tracking your thoughts and feelings throughout the day:** After writing your "positive download," you should feel energized, vibrant, and prepared to meet the day with enthusiasm and confidence. If you don't feel joyful and peaceful in any moment, identify the negative thought behind

it. Take the negative thought and flip it to the positive. Immediately look for the opportunity, lesson, acceptance, or gratitude that can emerge from whatever you're experiencing.

To put it mildly: This process is very powerful. Truth is, 50 percent of the time, we feel negative feelings. That's just how life is. We need to allow our feelings—good and bad—to rise up and pass. But when a negative thought grabs ahold, it's important to realize that it's here to teach you something to transform into a new way of being.

5. **Choose your reality:** You have a choice and get to decide what thoughts you want to have and how they get to govern your feelings. Check in with yourself when you aren't experiencing joy or lightness. Try it today, this week, for the next month, or for even longer.

Easily and gently ask yourself:

What am I thinking right now? What is the thought? And then, without giving the thought any meaning, without believing it, without making a big deal about it, or without resisting it, switch it to the positive. Even if it sounds delusional to be positive about everything, wouldn't you rather have joy and believe in the positive rather than believe anything else?

Loss

As someone who was adopted at birth, having a baby was fraught for me. Especially while I was going through infertility with my ex-husband.

Shlomi was a gentle, handsome six-foot-four and an ex–tank commander who had fought in the Lebanon war. His biceps were so large I could barely get my fingers around them. When we started dating in Los Angeles, he was thirty-two. I was thirty-four. We both wanted a family.

He was so much like my father. They had the same clever sense of humor. Both were hardworking salesmen running their own businesses. They were always positive, cheering me up. Dad took my cheeks into his hands and kissed my forehead. Shlomi did a "happy dance," shuffling his shoes on the living-room carpet, swinging his elbows. My siblings did a double take when Shlomi crossed his leg sideways, fidgeted with his wedding band, and grinned like Dad.

For our wedding in Los Angeles, a year after we met each other, Shlomi's family flew in from Tel Aviv and mine from Tulsa for the event. For a photograph after the ceremony, he raised me up, folding me in the crook of his arms. But at the party as we all danced to a big band, Dad wasn't his usual swinging self. He had found out he had lung cancer the day before our ceremony and kept it to himself. I felt so grateful that he and my mother walked me down the aisle before he fell ill.

Two years after our wedding, before my father's body broke down, he and my mother rented a simple one-bedroom apartment on the Santa Monica beach for the summer, right next to the pier, to be close to Shlomi and me. From their apartment window, we could see the Ferris wheel, and at sunset we would gather together for a glass of wine, which my father couldn't drink. Then, he would ride his Segway (my father loved his toys, and this was a fun way for him to get around without taxing his weak lungs) to the closest neighboring restaurant for Friday night Shabbat dinner. Nothing gave my father more pleasure than a good meal. He tried to stay positive as he told the waiter, "Nothing for me," because he had stopped eating entirely. All our eyes leaned toward our plates, knowing what he was losing. Yet, true to form, my father would order his favorite dessert regardless of his appetite: homemade butterscotch pudding with raw vanilla bean, and we would all share together without him in the remaining joy with long spoons. After one Friday night dinner, I put Glen Miller's "In the Mood" on speakers for Mom and Dad to have what would end up being their final swing dance together, as Shlomi and I took pictures of their smiling faces.

At the beginning of October, I went back to Tulsa to be with Dad for his last month. He dressed each morning: Mephisto walking shoes, khakis, and a knit sweater to sit in front of the television set and watch *M*A*S*H* reruns. Though his body was failing, it was important he could still "get up and at 'em."

I'd sit by him to keep him company and be near almost all day. We didn't talk much; he was too tired, but one afternoon out of nowhere, he told me, "I'm not worried about you because you have Shlomi. But I'd like to help you find your biological mother." Tying up his loose ends, Dad wanted me to find my own closures. He let me know he asked our family attorney to look into it, though it had been a closed adoption. It made me feel cared for that Dad understood I still had questions about my origin.

Shlomi met me in Tulsa each weekend at my parents' house, where I was staying. He sat with us as we watched *Cash Cab* together. He'd help lift Dad from his wheelchair into the bathroom. He picked Dad's whole weight up as we changed the sheets when my father could no longer move. My mother and brothers and I were moved to tears by Shlomi's care.

Even though there might not be anything harder than dealing with death, it was also a deep experience. Staying present during Dad's remaining time connected me profoundly to him as well as my family, and I cherished every lasting life moment. I wanted to meet Dad's passing, diving deeper with soulful inquiry:

- How could you look for every opportunity to love more, rather than exist in fear?

- How might you intend to face death and endings with courage?

- How could you appreciate every moment that brings you closer to a loved one, even while losing them, realizing that at the end of our lives all that matters is who we loved?

- How could the circumstances, no matter how difficult, be your greatest teacher?

- Could you use the whole experience, even the pain, as an opportunity to be more whole?

- Could you allow yourself to feel the loss and heartbreak but also honor all the love that was here?

When Dad passed at seventy-four years old, I was thirty-eight, and Shlomi and I were running out of time to have children. Getting pregnant was easy for me. My problem was keeping the baby. By my fourth miscarriage, each at around ten weeks, we stopped expecting to see a heartbeat on the monitor. Once, after I fell off the gynecologist's table onto my knees on the cold tile floor, Shlomi scooped me up with both arms. Another time I lost so much blood that he carried me to the car to take me back to the doctor's office. Another time, he toted the remains of our baby in a paper bag to a lab at Cedars Sinai to be tested as I waited in the car, still drugged and despondent.

Off and on for two years, I was on bed rest and told I shouldn't lift anything heavy, so Shlomi carried the groceries, my purse, and the UPS boxes inside. Frequently, he did his "happy dance" across the living-room floor. In sunken despair, I pulled a blanket over my head and curled up with Lita, our beloved Jack Russell terrier, the only baby I could have.

Then, every morning and evening, Shlomi patiently administered shots, but three fertility treatments failed. The doctor said, "Look into finding a donor." Defeated, Shlomi held my purse and helped me out of the office again.

"What about adopting?" I asked him.

"Let's look for a donor egg. Adoption would be my last option," he said.

"Is it because you want the child to be like you?"

He lowered his eyes, "Yes."

Shlomi was a traditional Middle Easterner. His family believed having the child was what brought happiness, a gift from above. I wanted to know that feeling too, the bond of a baby that was part of me. But as my mother always reminded me growing up, "You didn't grow under my heart, but in it."

When I received the news that the woman who gave birth to me was found, I wasn't prepared. Her name was Renee, and she wanted to speak to me right away. When the phone rang, Shlomi held my bouncing leg as he sat on the floor beside me.

"I've been looking for you. I've been waiting for you my whole life," she said.

"You have?"

"Yes, honey. You're my daughter. I gave birth to you," she said.

I had read many books on adoption, including one called *The Journey of the Adopted Self*, illuminating the adoptees' search for identity, particularly those who were part of the closed adoption system like Oklahoma when I was born. The book explained how closed-adoption adoptees were "betwixt and between." My confused identity issues combined with not being allowed to know where I was from made me feel like I couldn't belong anywhere, drifting.

On one hand I wanted her to love and want me, but on another, I had the only mother I wanted and didn't need another to replace her. "I would just like to get some answers about my history," I told her.

She willingly shared her story: Oddly, the first thing she said was that she gave birth to me on her birthday, September 2, and that she hadn't celebrated it since. I didn't like this. I wanted that day to be only mine, my special day to be celebrated. She told me my conception was a one-night stand when she was twenty. My biological father never knew about me. Later in life he committed suicide. I was relieved to fill in my missing puzzle pieces. I also asked her about my medical history and my birth, and I confided my problems having a baby.

"Why don't you just adopt? It seems that would be good for you. Maybe even important for your own healing," she said.

After the call, we friended each other on Facebook, and when I saw her pictures, I felt comforted that we looked like each other, the exact same eyes, mouth, and chin. However, I felt pressure to have to message her on our birthday after that, but I came to accept that I wanted bonding as an infant, and this was the one way I could safely connect. The rest of the time I kept my distance. I felt she wanted more than I could give.

I thought when I was married that having a family would provide me the identity I was seeking. Yet, working so hard to have one, I still felt like I wasn't me. Now that I had the answers I'd always wanted, I questioned everything: What if I didn't have a baby? Would that take the pressure off me? What if it didn't have to mean anything about me if I decided not to become a mother? What if I reneged on a commitment and a promise to Shlomi but stayed true to myself; could it be better for the both of us? Who did I want to be? And would Shlomi change with me?

I couldn't help but wonder why in this modern era I felt I didn't have any other choice than to be a mother—that that's what a woman should do by her late thirties. Who knows if I was just trying to please my husband, if it was my hormones, that crazy ticking biological clock, or if it was something I picked up from my Jewish ancestors? Even though my mother was raised in the 1950s, she never put any pressure on me to have children. She empowered me instead by insisting from the moment I graduated high school that it was my life, not about what she wanted, and that I should make my own decisions. And although she adored Shlomi, she did warn me when we first married about our cultural differences. I was starting to come to that realization. I did wonder if adopting a child might be healing, but I also knew that my happiness could come from another place rather than from giving birth to a baby.

Two years after Dad died, when I was forty, Mom was diagnosed with lymphoma when she was seventy. I flew back and forth from Los Angeles to Tulsa to help care for her. Yet, she still insisted I take our annual trip to Israel to be with Shlomi's family for the High Holidays. She knew how important it was for him.

One night, Shlomi and I went to a bar in Tel Aviv with his brother, who asked, "So when are you going to have children?"

"We've had a lot of trauma. I need a break," I said.

"You don't want kids?"

"I'm not sure right now." I evaded the question.

"You either want or you don't want. Which is it?" he asked in broken English.

"I don't," I said bluntly, angry he was asking.

"Did you just say you *don't* want children?" Shlomi asked, having overheard. "Get me another whiskey," he told the bartender in Hebrew.

After the two-week holiday, we flew back to my mother. "Well, this is the first time I've been comfortable around the two of you in years," Mom said, intuitively sensing, I think, that something major was different between Shlomi and me. It seemed the tension of the last few years had diminished. My decision had relieved the pressure. I suspected it also would be the final blow that ended our seven-year marriage.

"You've meant so much to me," Shlomi told my mother.

"You're going to make me cry. Don't say any more," she said with a Kleenex in her hand.

A month after Mom died, in November, Shlomi and I sat together at our back porch table in Los Angeles.

"I sense you're leaving," he said. "You never wanted to be a mother, did you?"

"I thought I did. But I've been unhappy."

"I've been unhappy too. I just didn't know it," he said, standing up. Always a man of a few words, he was finished with talking.

In December, he moved out. In January, we signed the divorce papers. In February, I called to tell him Lita was dying and needed to be put down. He rushed over. He found me curled on the couch holding our terrier.

"Take the time you need. We don't have to rush to take her in," Shlomi said as he went to the kitchen to pour a glass of water and brought it back to me.

He helped me wrap her in her white snuggly blanket. He placed her in my embrace in the passenger seat and drove us to the hospital. The doctor came in. With Lita on my lap, her head resting on my thigh, I adjusted in my seat so all three of us could get more comfortable.

"Shlomi, scoot over," I said softly and felt his body press to my side. He put his arm around me so we could be a family, as I knew it, for the last time.

· ·

Letting go of my marriage as well as choosing not to have children at forty-two years old was extremely difficult. I worried that I left a life that could never be replaced. I feared loneliness and dying alone. I wrote in my journal for hours every day, trying to make sense of my life. I was surprised by how my creative juices got flowing after such loss, but I was appreciative. Writing was another way I pulled through. Rather than a baby, I chose creativity. For certain, it was another kind of life force. I allowed myself to deeply explore my past story and the wound in order to heal it. To let go of my past, I chose to write my life out and rewrite and rewrite until it was healed.

I used creativity as my savior through my grief and darkness, whether that was creative writing, painting, or how I made concerted decisions to create the life I wanted—one of joy, love, and interconnectedness. Without the steadfast ability to tap into my creativity and my trust in it, I might not have gotten through. The creative outlet I chose needn't have been literally writing the story of my life down to get to the other side of my story. But it was and it helped.

With each journal entry I came closer to my truth. With each new page, I reached a place of forgiveness and compassion. When I finally came to no longer being emotionally triggered by the material I was writing, I knew I was returning to my heart and love for those I was writing about and myself. Today, I don't even know who that woman was I wrote about. She was a phantom wandering through the landscape of a distant dream. I can remember her with fondness, but it's no longer me.

A Healing Journal Activity

1. Write the story of a loss you have had, or a transition you are going through— whatever that is, be it the end of a relationship, the death of a loved one, the loss of a job, etc. Be truthful about how you feel. Raw. Go to the places you fear, or feel anger, pain, hurt, or grief. Express yourself fully.

2. Imagine you are on your own deathbed. How would you want to remember this story? Are there places within it that have yet to be healed? What would it take to find resolve? What might you want to say to another in order to die with no regrets, connected fully in your loving? Write these answers down. Explore them fully.

3. Close your eyes and imagine the other person. State out loud to yourself as many times as you need until you feel a deep release:

    I'm sorry.

    Please forgive me.

    I love you.

    Thank you.

4. Keeping your eyes closed, see *yourself* at the time this loss happened. State out loud to yourself as many times as you need until you feel a deep release:

    I'm sorry.

    Please forgive me.

    I love you.

    Thank you.

5. Now, rewrite the story. Bring it into the light. Flood it with positive energy. Remove any blame or judgment. Come to it with kindness, acceptance, and compassion. Find gratitude and appreciative joy for another and yourself.

6. Keep recreating writing this story until it is fully completed within you and you feel whole. It might take a progression over time. But as you do it you will find the pieces that hold pain lift away. And you will be freed for good.

Loneliness

Like a caring mother holding and guarding the life of her only child, so with a boundless heart of loving kindness, hold yourself and all beings as your beloved children.

—Buddha

After all the losses, when loneliness haunted me, I was flooded with memories of being lonely as a little a girl. My mother didn't like me to have friends over all that much, and I spent a lot of time in my room, listening to records and playing with my stuffed animals.

At bedtime as a small child, my brother Russ listened to his stereo with headphones or talked with truckers on his CB with his door closed. My brother Marty hung out in his room with guy friends, readying to go out to a party.

Russ's stereo would send the faint sound of seventies rock music back to my orange-papered room, papered that way because it was mother's favorite color. Marty would rush out the door to go to his disco party.

I would hug my giant-sized stuffed gorilla named Rootbeer, and ask him to protect me, always in a whisper because I was afraid my parents would overhear. I closed my eyes, opened them halfway, and peered through them to make the ceiling blur. I didn't want to sleep because I knew what was awaiting me in my dream: a giant spider spinning its web high on top of the bed frame.

"Rootbeer, it's back," I murmured into his ear.

Hairy and ugly, the spider spoke to me in a shrill hi-fi voice like an electric drill that penetrated my skull, its white, sharp teeth visible through a shrieking black mouth.

I shoved Rootbeer off me and jumped out of bed, taking my "blankey" and my pillow, dragging them to the open door, and curling up in a ball inside the doorframe. My toes spread against one side of the open doorway's frame, the side of my head against the other. I wanted to be near the hall light, to be near the sound of my grown-up family so I could feel a part of them.

I closed my eyes tight, hoping to squeeze out the voice of the spider above my bed. I held my blankey against my cheek and rested a corner of it on my lips. Hiding my thumb in my mouth behind it, I finally slept.

In the morning, I woke up in my bed with Rootbeer on top of me. Marty must have put us there when he got home from being with his friends. No one asked me in the morning why I slept in the doorway. If they had, I wouldn't have told them it was because of the spider.

The spider's piercing voice echoed in my ears and continued well into adulthood. When the creature spoke, it reminded me of the horror, the shame, and where my self-hatred came from: "You are no good. You will never be perfect. You will never be enough."

Inner voices like these can haunt us and separate us from our sense of connection and love. The only reason why they do is because we believe them.

But when experiencing an innate sense of loneliness after the losses, I knew one important thing: I had lost connection to my creativity. To overcome the stuck, low feelings of self-judgment and criticism, I knew that I needed to get busy working on my greater life dreams. I immediately started asking myself questions to feel connected again:

- What do I really want in life?
- What and how do I want to learn?
- What would be fun right now to explore?
- What excites me, interests me, or makes me feel alive?
- If I could do anything, if my possibilities were infinite, what would I create?

When I was connected to something I was passionate about, I never felt alone. And as a bonus, I forgot all that negative stuff I was telling myself because I was too busy doing what turned me on and was fun.

To feel even more connected, I thought about how I wanted to give back to others. How I would like to make a difference. How I might make the world a better place. I investigated my strengths and how I wanted to expand upon them.

I learned a powerful lesson during that time: There was a difference between loneliness and aloneness.

Loneliness stems from a wound, a place of feeling separation: a place of neediness and a need for attention. It's not wrong that we feel lonely; there's just a way to reframe it. Aloneness is a place for solitude: a powerful and profound time to develop a relationship with yourself. In solitude, you have the space, time, and energy to know yourself more intimately and have a romantic affair with your own heart. You develop more understanding of who you are and who you are not in order to move to the next level in yourself and in your relationships. You gain more clarity on how you choose to relate with the world. You restore, replenish, and recoup. You relinquish what no longer serves, and download new, updated programs to begin anew.

Loneliness feels like a void, like a black hole that might suck you in. But aloneness is quite the opposite. It's not a place where you lose yourself. It's a place in which you gain. A place of expansion, a widening of the heart, a deepening of your wisdom, and the reception of insight—all of which are limitless and infinite. Each and every time you go through a period of solitude, you come out of it so much stronger, empowered, capable, less needy, less grasping . . . whole.

The energy of relationships moves in a current, like a figure eight: We come together and we move apart. We come together and we move apart again. When we love the distances as much as the togetherness, we've learned how to love others and ourselves more.

During a profound amount of years of solitude, I learned that nothing outside me could make me feel loved, safe, and cared for. Nothing outside me could resolve my fear. I knew that loving myself meant—with time—I would come to trust that I could care for and fulfill my own needs. I learned to make new choices to help discover step by step how to decrease any suffering. I knew deep within that the love and joy that was mine to create would magnetize love and joy outside me once I held my own heart first. Any and all self-loving actions I took would speed up the process of creating what I really wanted in my life.

What I discovered was that it was all an illusion; this belief that I was "alone" didn't exist. It was just a sham. I reached a deep sense of inner compassion. I loved giving myself permission to not be hard on myself and not judge myself for how I was growing or any perceived failings on my part. That compassion is what set me free. Free to be me. Free to accept myself with all of my various issues and quirky qualities. That in turn allowed me to be more compassionate toward others in my life in the same way I was for me. I no longer felt the need to control or change anything, and I could just live the magnificent life creativity intended for me. I didn't have to have it all figured out.

When I was counseling in my late thirties, after I got my master's in counseling psychology, before every session with a client I'd take a few minutes to center myself in myself. I'd invoke my Highest Self to come forward and I'd say: *May this session be for the highest good of all concerned.* I imagined in my mind's eye that I was a channel for whatever was for the best for our session, for my client, for me, and for our relationship to come through me. Then, I could get out of the way. My mind could take a side seat. I wouldn't have to force things or feel pressured to find answers, and I'd be relieved from "performance anxiety." Getting out of my head, I didn't have to believe I had to be doing or saying the right thing. Instead, I could just be present with whatever arose, ready to meet it fully.

When we think *I'm doing this* and become self-conscious, rather than just allowing the energy to move through us, we can get caught in our own heads. Like when we self-reference, making it all about us, rather than really seeing, hearing, and feeling the other person we are trying to connect with. We tighten up rather than relax into an organic and authentic flow of engagement. We may think we have to contribute more than just listening, loving, or having compassion. But sometimes our simple listening presence is all that's needed for the other beside us to figure out what they need. We try to fix, give advice, or problem solve, and that never does anyone any good, because ultimately we all must learn for ourselves. True insight is found within each individual for lasting change.

I used to think it was my job to take on other people's problems, especially in my closest relationships. I did it because I didn't want to be abandoned. If I could fix them, change them, or make them into something greater, then they wouldn't leave me. But every single time I tried to control, I ended up pushing those I loved away rather than creating the closeness I craved.

As an empathetic, feeling, intuitive being I can "feel" the people around me, especially those I care about and love the most. It was hard for me not to get involved in what others were doing. I wanted to make things better when I saw someone else in pain or having difficulty, rather than focus on my own. But I learned it wasn't my job to take on what another person needed to carry. It wasn't my business.

What if:

- We didn't fight another's battle for them?
- We let them figure out things for themselves to find their own empowerment?
- We didn't try to control another to reap a benefit?

But what do we do when we're feeling stuck and emotionally drained from a past relationship that we've lost? When we fear being alone? When it's hard to move on because for some reason we can't let go of another, no matter how hard we try? When we're scared we're not going to find someone else, or have a family, or feel truly loved?

You know that feeling when you put your hand on a hot stove and it burns, but you keep doing it anyway? You walk by the stove, and you think: *I don't know what else to do, so I'll just put my hand there.* And you keep hurting yourself, not knowing how to get out of the loop. You still place it on the stove and think, *That hurts!* And then you put it on the stove again and think, *Yep, it still hurts.* One day you walk by the stove and think, *I know it's going to hurt, but just because that's what I'm used to doing, I'm going to put my hand there once more.* And then one day, you walk by the stove and think, *Nope, I don't want to do that anymore.*

Realizing that we don't want to put our hand on the stove is the first crucial step. But breaking patterns isn't easy, and since we're human, it's unreasonable to think our habits can change overnight. That's why it takes us a few times (sometimes more than we care to admit) where we continue to burn our hand until we just come to a place of being sick of it.

What seems to take us longer to understand is the confusion we feel around the pain of feeling lonely. Even though our heart tells us we would be better off if we made more self-loving choices, our mind makes us think the opposite.

Isn't our mind funny? It grasps on to something that causes us pain, because that's what it has become accustomed to. It figures *a hot stove is better than nothing.*

It doesn't believe there could be less pain if we went another direction. In fact, it protects us because it believes there will be more of it.

The truth is, there's always a less painful option. And that option, if made from a self-loving place, will bring better returns.

But how do you let go?

Take the hand that's on the hot stove and place it on your heart. Nothing outside you can make you feel loved, safe, cared for, and connected. Nothing outside you will absolve your fear. Only your heart's love for yourself and health can stop you from causing self-harm.

Loving yourself means that—with time—you can come to trust that you can care for and fulfill your own needs. You can make new choices to help you discover step by step how to decrease your suffering.

Then something awesome happens.

Every time you walk by the stove, you get more ready—ready to have what you want more fully. You become stronger to share your life with someone not as a completion, but as an addition to you.

The love and joy you create within will magnetize love and joy outside you once you make your own heart first. Because it's then you know how you went through the fire and learned how not to get burned. Any and all self-love actions you take will speed up the process of creating more of what you want.

Intimacy means INTO ME I SEE. When we desire intimacy, we have opportunity to see into our own self—rather than want others to fill in us all the things we feel we're lacking. In our desire to create the relationships we want, it's our responsibility to make the changes in our own life, and thus, we affect the other lives we touch as well.

We all want closeness in varying degrees. And depending on daily-life circumstances, we want different things. Yet, at times we act out certain patterns in our various needs for security.

We can be anxious, cling, act needy, dependent, complain, or nag. We grasp, wanting the other to relieve our fear of rejection, abandonment, lack of self-love, or loneliness.

We can be avoidant, pushing away, shutting down, criticizing, being passive, or refusing to communicate. We find other things to put our attention on, like work, addictions, other people, or other things.

We can be ambivalent. Depending on how we feel, we can flip between anxious and avoidant—all due to the uncertainties of intimacy. We either crave closeness and control or cut off, perhaps unconsciously.

And last, *we can be secure*, be safe in closeness, and also have loving boundaries with compassion when we need space for ourselves.

Oh, how I wished I were more secure at times in my past. But in truth, it's normal and natural in relationships to be anxious, avoidant, or ambivalent. A purpose, if not the biggest purpose on this Earth, is to learn how not to be afraid of love. As I witnessed the deaths of my parents, I noticed that there was one common theme. When facing their final moments, neither cared about what they had accumulated over their lifetime. In the heightened presence of meeting their last breaths, their perspective changed. What really mattered was not what they accomplished or owned. What mattered most above all else was who loved them and whom they loved.

If you tend toward anxiousness, the trick is to rest in the discomfort of spaciousness without needing someone else to complete you, and fill it with your own self-nurturing. If you lean toward the avoidant, it's important to be aware of your fear of closeness; step toward and open up, to take a risk to receive, soften your heart, and let love in.

Obviously, there are relationships where there is too-much dependency or too wide of a gap—where the other is no longer present. When this happens, therapy is a good thing. Or perhaps, an acceptance is needed that things have come to an end, and then making the necessary arrangements to leave the relationship as lovingly as you can.

There's this story about a horse in a large field. He has his favorite place grazing in a corner. If you put a fence around him, nine times out of ten he bucks up. If you take the fence down, chances are you still find him peacefully chewing in his corner. The same goes with relationship. One-two-three, one-two-three, we waltz. You step forward. I step back. But in each other's embrace we dance.

I used to think that the people I was in a relationship with were there to give me my happiness rather than add to it. It took me years to realize I had so many opportunities to live my own full life, so that at the end of the day I had so much more to share. I couldn't rely on my partners, family members, or friends to shift my moods, heal me, or fill my empty spaces. It wasn't my responsibility to do that for them either. Support is an integral part of any human connection. We're there on the bad days with compassion and a loving embrace. We're there on the good days to cheer. But mostly, I needed to rely on myself to give that love to myself, and solitude was what was needed.

I learned in my alone time that it wasn't someone else's job to give me what I want. It was mine. I had the opportunity to see what I really wanted and then create that for myself: If I wanted more *passion*, then I had an opportunity to be more passionate. If I wanted more *love*, then I had an opportunity to be more loving to another and myself. If I wanted more *compassion*, then I had an opportunity to be more compassionate with others and myself. If I wanted more *fun and happiness*, then I had an opportunity to create more joy for myself. If I wanted more *attention*, then I had an opportunity to attend to my own needs.

Too often I thought: *Aren't THEY supposed to fix everything?* Uh, nope. I wanted to manipulate my relationships to have what I was unable to give to another or myself. In the end, what it came down to was me. My empowerment came from being the person I wanted the other to be in relationship.

I tried to control my loves and our environment as a way to feel safe and protected. I finally realized that the only thing needed was for me to be in my heart and care, to never try to change anything about another person's experience or attempt to take that away from them. It's not my job to heal another. It's my job to let them wrestle with themselves. That's the only way we all learn and grow, by reaching our own individual conclusions. It took forever, but I finally got it. Rather than see how I could change another, my priority became about what I needed to change in me.

The intention of stating *for the highest good of all concerned* before each counseling session also became my intention in life. Our Higher Self could represent Divinity, Nature, Soul, Enlightenment, or religious names for God. A friend described it this way: Stillness and Loving. I just think of it as Love. But whatever it is, it's something that transcends us into an unlimited connection with the force of the universe, a place of warmth, kindness, and goodness. Space where permission is given for all to be present, somewhere that's boundless and more vast than the smallness of our personality that thinks it's the one in charge.

For me, it's the same for all creative endeavors—whether that's art, business, manifesting dreams, resolving personal issues, or how we go about our day-to-day work, caring for our children and relationships. When we're centered, we're in tune with our intuition. That intuition becomes our inspiration. And what inspires us creates expansion. The more we expand, the more acceptance there is. The more we accept what's in front of us, the less we need to control or avoid it. The less we need to control or avoid it, the more we get out of our own way. Getting out of our way, we realize it isn't about us. And when we realize it isn't about us, the more we Love and let Love in.

That's why I'm passionate about the creative process. And why I think everything we do is creative. Because when we're in tune to what we're creating with a sense of Love, we reach our greatest fulfillment.

Embracing Your Solitude and Making the Most of It

1. Create a conscious, mindful retreat for yourself at home. Find a couple of days, perhaps the weekend, to turn off the phones, not write emails, forget technology or the TV, and let people know you are taking some time off. Do what you need to do to have the experience of retreat. Meet yourself fully in your solitude.

2. How will you create this without interruption? What would a period of solitude look like for you? What healthy foods would you prepare to sustain you? What would you need to do to set this up so that you will not be distracted?

3. Where could you find nature for this retreat? Is there a hike, garden, or quiet path to sit, walk, and reflect?

4. How do you anticipate this experience of solitude will support you? What do you feel you will gain from it on an inner and outer level? Set an intention in order to create your best experience.

5. Could you spend some time on this retreat focusing on what you love most about yourself? Intend to raise your heart space up, and expand your love for yourself, your life, and all your many blessings. Make this your focus— you loving you at your highest capacity and appreciating every single heartbeat.

6. After having your experience of retreat, explore what you've learned and what it gave you in your journal. Do you feel more empowered? How has this experience strengthened you? Do you feel calmer, less afraid, more connected inwardly and self-loving?

Play

Grown-ups never understand anything by themselves, and it's exhausting for children to have to provide explanations over and over.

—Antoine De Saint-Exupery

The first time I painted, my world exploded. I was twenty-eight years old, and I remember dipping bristles into vivid blue pigment and smoothing them over a sheet of white paper pinned to the wall. I'd never picked up a brush. Never in my wildest dreams did I think I could be a painter. I couldn't draw. I always wanted to when I was a child, but repeated in my notebook the same one doodle of a flower.

Yet, my whole life I had been searching for ways I could express myself. I loved acting as a kid and doing school plays. Later, I got a BFA in theater. I always loved writing and wrote all the time even when I didn't think I could ever be good enough to be a published writer. But painting? No. That was something I never envisioned.

When I was twenty-eight, a writing teacher of mine, Natalie Goldberg, author of *Writing Down the Bones*, suggested I attend a painting workshop taught by Michele Cassou, author of *Life, Paint and Passion*. Since Natalie pushed, I gave in and reluctantly went.

The painting workshop was held in Taos, New Mexico, at the Mabel Dodge Luhan House. The beige adobe was covered with white boards and individual pieces of four-by-five-foot sheets of white, cold-press artist's paper thumbtacked to the wall. Two long tables sat in the middle of the room. Rows of colorful, thick tempera paint in clear plastic cups were laid out on them like lines of treasure. Next to each color of paint was an individual cup of water and a large French Isabey brush.

The teacher, Michele, a petite woman with a small, sharp nose, intense brown eyes, and a strong Parisian accent, told us to go to a color that drew us, dip the brush into the water and then into the paint, and go to our paper. The only instruction we were given: "*To play*." That way, we'd stay open to spontaneity, adventure, and the unexpected.

Never having held a paintbrush before, I was told not to grasp it too tightly and keep my wrist relaxed. I will never forget the very first time my brush made contact. When my fingers held the lacquered, full-bodied brush handle with the right amount of water and paint, and the color of deep-ocean blue I had picked glided across smooth white paper, all my senses awakened. My stroke came alive. I fell in love. Still to this day, after over twenty years of painting, my heart cracks wide open when I first begin by choosing a color that draws me, and laying the paint onto a clean sheet.

But that first day, I was nervous. What would I paint if I didn't know how to draw an image?

"*Play!*" Michele told us in her loud, energizing French accent.

I felt like a child who only knew how to draw stick figures. I was worried and already embarrassed the other workshop attendees would think my painting would look like a kindergartner's. But I let my brush move and then went back to the table to choose a different color. This time I chose magenta.

"Keep moving!" Michelle called out excitedly. "Between paper and table. By physically moving you are more in your body and less in your head."

Because I had the excuse of never having painted before, I decided that I didn't have to care what anyone else thought. I could play like I was told and was thrilled to be given unlimited permission to unleash my wild, creative self.

Every few minutes, Michele threw a question out to the room. Questions like, what if:

- You could take a risk?
- It didn't matter what it looked like?
- There was nothing to lose?

The entire notion turned me on. I mean, *What if I applied those same questions to my life?* I made it my mission to discover and to work with these questions on deeper levels.

Twenty years later, I still have that very first painting. It did look like a kindergartner's, but I love it because it was the very moment I started on my artistic adventure. I keep it with my hundreds of other paintings from over the years, catalogued in order by date, underneath my bed. A friend said to me once, "You're going to keep painting until your bed reaches the stars!" I've never forgotten that.

I learned from that first workshop that the most essential way to create any life desire is to begin with play. Isn't this a great way to approach something new? When starting any project or change of life course, we must begin somehow.

What might you begin without care or worry? What have you longed to do but haven't tried? Ride a motorcycle across the desert through Montana's mountains? Find another job with more pay that will make you happier? Move to a place that's quieter? Plant a garden? Clean out your closets and redecorate? Learn to play guitar?

Our inner judge may attempt to tell us why we can't have the impulse to be free. Whether spending too long to create a business plan or making lists, to the extreme of only writing lists rather than doing them. We can have a tendency to take a ruler and projector and draw all the lines first before we color them in. We look ahead and try to decide what we have to do to make an entire project, dream, or career move come true. We think we can govern how what we want to create will look in the end. But in the very beginning, this only sets us up for doom. It can actually stop us from beginning in the first place because we don't give ourselves permission to begin. What if:

- When beginning anything new, you simply allowed yourself to play?

- It didn't matter what it looked like?

- Anything could happen without care or worry?

- You were free? I mean, really?

- You were open to all possibilities?

Play is how we step into discovery with curiosity. Here, you are free from the limitations. You get to be childlike again, where you don't care about what other people think and enter into the dream world that is ready to open up to you.

- If you were to play, simply play, how might you enter your experience differently than how you might have previously?

- What might you explore more of just for the hell of it?
- When you showed up to work or your household tasks with the essence of play, might you do it with less stress?
- Or rather than approaching something with the assumption that this will be a drag, instead you looked for ways you could enjoy it?

With permission to play in that workshop in the dry, dusty New Mexico desert, I could paint whatever I wanted. I could use any color I wanted. I didn't have to identify myself as being anything—especially a painter. I could just paint as a beginner.

What would you do without care or worry without previous experience, or no specific goal in mind? You don't have to know the outcome at the beginning. You don't have to know where it's going. Or what will happen next. You don't have to have all your questions answered. You can treat it as a fun adventure.

What aliveness would this invoke in you? What might you do? Perform at your first open-mic night? Start up your dream consulting business? Go solo on a plane? Add more lightness and humor to your life?

Sometimes when I had an idea about something I wanted to write, I put it off, waiting for the structure from beginning to end to be clear. Then I remembered my painting process and reminded myself that I could have that special moment again with a blank sheet of paper. I let myself be surprised by what thoughts rose up that I hadn't thought of before, and I reminded myself when beginning, whether a new project or life aspiration, or even when I awoke each morning, that this was a great way to approach *everything*.

Your intuition will tell you what is calling you right now in order to invoke an essence of play.

- Without analyzing it, without thinking about it, where would your wishes start?
- Could you start for the pure intention of exploration without having to know the end product?
- Could you be spontaneous?
- Could you make choices, step by step, based only on what is in front of you?

I'm so grateful for that first painting workshop. Now, when it comes to my painting process (and life), anything and everything is possible. Painting is my safe space, and that makes me very happy. Sometimes, when I find I want to curl up into a ball and hide, take a long nap, or rage or cry, I gently nudge myself to pick up my brush and meet the paper head on instead.

It's cathartic, sure. But it's more than that. For me, it's like an active meditation, enabling me to use painting as a way to wake up to my life's endless possibilities. It doesn't matter why a particular image wants to come through or what it signifies. I paint with wonder, allowing my brush to take me in the direction it chooses. After all, these paintings are less about me and more about getting out of my own way so that the current of creativity can come through.

Without consciously trying, each image exposes the curves, swirls, and edges of my life. Dipping my brush into paint and sliding the bristles across paper, I feel connected to something far greater than me. Regardless of the image, dark or light, I feel energetic, awake, high. What I hold in my perception becomes more alive. I'm content, open, and present, and I need to do nothing more than meet paper with color.

Today, I remind myself of the simplicity in every new beginning: What if in life, with any endeavor I wanted to begin, I just took one step, like going to the table and choosing one color? And then, placed it against paper? Then, when I felt called, I went to the next color and then another?

Creative freedom and play go hand in hand. As kids you took risks without even thinking. Like doing somersaults down a grass hill with green stains and mud all over you, even if your parents worried you would break your neck. You didn't map out the exact physics it would take to roll down the hill, to make sure you missed a pothole and didn't end up on the concrete below. You didn't calculate the speed of the somersault to make sure you had enough momentum to not stop in the middle.

Nah, you just rolled.

Sure, you got bumps and bruises and cuts along the way, because that's how we play.

The point is to be childlike as you begin something new. To be simply curious about what might come out of you.

Every time you do something new, like a first cartwheel, it's a thrilling experience. You do it for the sheer joy. Isn't that why you want to begin something new in the first place?

Many times what you did as a child or loved as a child can reconnect you to your purpose and passions. When you were a child, were you ever accused of as being "too much"? For example: You're too impatient, too detailed, too opinionated, too sensitive, too introverted or extroverted, too shy, too loud, too weird, etc. Were you ever reprimanded for being "annoying"?

It may feel like these childhood "flaws" are far behind you, but don't underestimate how these experiences might also offer a clue about your unique gifts and talents. They might reveal what's calling to you right now.

As a child, my mother often felt I was "too much." I was sometimes discouraged about my passions. But today, I see my "too much" as my superpower.

In fifth grade, on one of my father's business trips to Manhattan, my parents decided to bring me along. Mom asked my father if he would get us tickets to see my first Broadway musical, *Annie*. I'm not sure if it crossed my mother's mind that the story was about an adoptee and how much it might influence me at eleven years old. Sarah Jessica Parker starred. I wore the suit my mother had bought me back home: a plaid red, black, and yellow pleated skirt with a short red wool jacket with gold buttons, white tights, and patent leather shoes. It was all topped off with my grandfather's red beret sitting at a slant on my petite head.

My father rented a limousine as a special treat. It pulled up in front of the theater, the sidewalk filled with ticket holders. As the driver got out of the car and opened my door, the crowd turned, saw my patent leather shoes, my legs reach to touch the sidewalk, and when they saw the red suit emerge, with a young girl in it, they started to applaud. I thought the welcoming was because of the limousine. I didn't realize they thought I was Annie.

That was the moment I fell in love with the theater. I returned to Tulsa singing the songs from the musical out loud on the playground at recess. At Thanksgiving dinner, arms stretched out and fingers extending full force, I practically screamed the lyrics of "The Sun Will Come Out Tomorrow" for my entire family.

My twenty-one-year-old brother, Marty, who was a theater major at Northwestern then, did a drum roll on his knees for me. Mom closed her eyes, sticking her fingers into her ears, begging me to stop because I was so loud. But I kept singing.

In fifth grade I performed in my first play as Nori in *The Hobbit*. In seventh grade, I was the Red Queen in *Alice in Wonderland*. And in eighth grade, the Wicked Witch in *The Wizard of Oz*. The theater became my place for self-expression. On the stage, I was free!

Today, I still hold this little Lynn close within me. I make it my goal to stay true to my expression as much as I can and share myself openly.

- What's your childhood "too much"?

- How might you use it to find and strengthen your superpower?

- Where might this lead you to fully engage your passions and purpose?

Creativity is life making. It's anything you do that turns you on, invigorates you, or offers a simple moment of pure merriment. Because after all, the greatest art created is a truly lived life.

All of us have something we enjoy doing. Or something we think we would enjoy but don't do because the bigger, more-pressing things in our daily lives take priority. We just don't make the time for it. Or we judge it as "a little hobby" (like crafting, kickball, or learning magic tricks). Or we think it will never become something significant or important (like changing the world). Or we deem it as just plain silly. (Why pick up singing when we don't even know how to stay in harmony?) But what we enjoy is far more important than we could ever realize, and can make a significant impact on our lives.

As a kid you could create anything and have fun with it without worrying about what other people thought. Creativity returns you to the innocence of your childhoods. And giving yourself a break from the pressures of adulthood, you become lighter and increase your sense of humor as you delight in the pleasure of your amusements. You're led to new, wonderful, unexpected opportunities.

But even more, the current of creativity always leads you to bigger life experiences and realizations. Even a small creative project might open you to whole new possibilities. You never know where it might lead, and in that unknown outcome is an important freedom.

The fastest, most instantaneous way to shake the energy up when you get stuck is to have some fun with your child self. (Right now *my* inner child wants to take a pot and hit a pan and run all around the room, screaming INNER CHILD INNER CHILD INNER CHILD INNER CHILD—just because it sounds that ridiculous . . .) But if you think about it, it does make sense. When were you the happiest, most playful, not-caring-what-anyone-thought, get-your-hands-dirty, little human? Isn't that the part of you that really knows how to let go and have fun?

When I'm feeling stuck, I ask my child self what she wants to do, and schedule a play date with myself. Hello . . . instant fun! But there's also a rule I have when I do it (you know how kids need rules). As I go on this "date," I don't think about what other things I need to do or get done or think about anything at all, actually. I just enjoy. Remember fun?

To overcome my grief, I tried to take myself on a play date at least once a week, like going to see some theater, taking a walk at a park, meeting up with girlfriends and laughing, or sitting in a café and watching people. It totally gave me energy, shifted up my mood, and helped to refresh me. Not to mention it added playful energy to all the other hard, mundane, difficult things I was dealing with.

What does your little self want to do? Maybe he or she wants to ride a bike, take a pottery/dance/improv class, dig up dirt in your garden, sit in the grass, bake cupcakes, ride a Ferris wheel, go to a car show, or visit a fire station and talk with the firemen. It's all about making our kid self happy. And when *they're* happy, *we're* happy, so why not find a reason to laugh and be silly? You know, that funny little thing that makes us giggle, chuckle, throw our hands in the air, do a jig, cover our mouths, or bellow. It's a great way to deal with an upset too. Like, in the middle of a conflict, it might seem rude to break out into laughter. But it's an icebreaker. Somehow, it just makes everything okay and puts it *all* into perspective.

ACTIVITY
Invoke the Playful Side of You

1. **What's something you've always wanted to do but never took the time to try?** What would you do, right now, if you had permission to do what interests you, even if it may sound ridiculous? What if you created a new experience? The more you engage, the more your spirits fly. The more you nurture your dreams, the more your light shines. Do you want to run a marathon? Learn to ice skate? Write a novel? Learn to meditate? Travel to your bucket list place?

2. **Schedule a play date.** Commit to doing one small thing to begin. For example, download a couch-to-5K app, spend a Saturday afternoon at the rink, read a book on meditation, research travel opportunities, or create a Pinterest board of your favorite places.

3. **Whatever you choose to do—do it with the essence of play.** Just for the fun of it. With no greater purpose except to add joy and enthusiasm.

4. **Put in your calendar what you will do each week to continue.** Even if it's a half hour a week. There is always time to add a bit of fun into your life. Not having time is never an excuse. Make yourself your greatest priority.

Seeds

> *You were designed for accomplishment, engineered for success, and endowed with the seeds of greatness.*
>
> —Zig Ziglar

When I first studied creative writing in my midtwenties with Natalie Goldberg, she had us write for ten minutes, keeping our hands moving, not crossing out or editing as we wrote. This stream of consciousness allowed the creative exploration without interruption or interpretation. We had permission to allow whatever wanted to arise. After the timer went off, she had us read what we wrote out loud to the group, with an important rule to follow: *No comments.*

Many times what I wrote and shared with the group emerged from an emotional and vulnerable place inside, without inhibition. Like the title of Natalie's first bestselling book, *Writing Down the Bones*, my bare, raw bones were exposed. If it weren't for the rule of "no comments," my freedom of expression may not have flowed out of me. Like a newborn, we need to wait some time before presenting our infant free of contaminants to the outside world. But in a safe workshop environment with the rule of no comments, I could keep my vulnerable expressions coddled, safe, and warm.

Let's say you want to plant your own vegetable garden. You dig a hole, add plenty of organic matter, rake it smooth, and then plant each individual seed. You also know you need to protect it from the elements and the critters, so you put stakes around it and foil on top to keep it from the sun. You lay out netting to keep away the birds and cover it with mulch to keep the soil moist because seeds sprout much faster from warm soil. Just like planting a garden, you realize when creating something new that you have opportunity to treat it like a baby seedling.

Keeping what you want to create protected and close when beginning something brand new is essential because you're birthing from a sacred, connected place. If you allow other energies, people, opinions, feedback, or comments, you can expose your creative inner world to pathogens and infection. Too often when you're just beginning, the opinions of others can freeze your blooming essence.

When we ask for comments from others on what we're newly creating, we can internalize their perceptions. As much as we don't like to admit it, if we care too much about what other people think, it affects us. There's a time to get outside impressions—they can be helpful for us to see what we might not have otherwise been able to know on our own. But it's most helpful once the stem is strong enough to stand against the wind's blows to bend and not break.

A friend of mine got a great idea for a documentary about medical aid workers in Uganda. She was excited about it. She had a sense of what it could be about, interviewed contacts, did her research, took a trip to Africa, and started writing. But after she wrote a first draft she gave it to someone she knew in the entertainment business, who gave her a lot of overwhelming feedback. She stopped writing for a little while.

Another friend, after going through a difficult breakup, got an idea for a blog to support people with relationship hardships. She had a catchy name and a great logo, but after she wrote a few blog posts and didn't get a lot of comments, she put it on hold.

A third friend, who was in the beauty business, had a dream of creating her own skin-care line. She wanted to know what she was going to call it before she began. She thought of a brand name she really liked and started asking people what they thought of it. With everyone's different opinions, I watched her initial enthusiasm wither.

It's important to not ask anyone for feedback right away and to trust ourselves enough to begin without another's validation. If we keep it to ourselves for a little while until we feel more confident, we won't shoot it up into the sky and then pop the air out of it.

My friend who was writing the documentary took a month off but then went back to her project, far more cautious about sharing it. When we spoke about it, I made sure never to ask her about the specifics of the storyline. I spoke with her only about her writing process when she wanted support to keep going.

My other friend went back to writing more consistently, committing to a blog post once a week. Within a year, people were sharing her words on social media and she developed a nice following.

My third friend did start up her beauty line a few months later. She wrote a business plan and created a sample. One day a brand name came to her that felt so right, she didn't have the need to ask anyone about it.

A project in its early stages needs preservation and nurturing. After all, we don't take our newborns out into the world and let everyone touch them. We keep them swaddled, close to our heart, and sheltered.

All feedback is "bad" feedback in the beginning. If someone says, "*Wow! That's the greatest idea I've heard in a long time. It's so funny. This is sure to be an Oscar winner!*," then the pressure is on to make it so. That pressure could switch you off. It doesn't mean it will, but it could. So why not carefully protect your dreams?

If someone says, "*You know, that's a good idea, but what if you did so-and-so or that reminds me of this other movie I saw . . . ,*" or any comment positive or negative, you can get blocked, sometimes permanently.

And the worst thing is, when you don't care what anyone else says about it, but you comment on it *yourself.* Talking too much about a project in the beginning can put you in your head. Rather than allow your intuition to download for you, you can spend it, depleting the flow of the creative current. Feedback can cause you to lose the gift of the unsullied, pure original thought that rouses from your imagination.

This goes for everything you begin. Not just creative projects. Like when you tell your friends about a new person you're dating, and suddenly everyone starts having an opinion, or asking questions, and you lose the purity of the budding romance. Or you talk too much about how you want to have more passion in your relationship rather than just taking the hand of your beloved and embracing them. Or you find out you're pregnant, and every woman you tell in your community wants to tell you the "correct" way to carry out your birth plan. Keeping your seeds to yourself in the beginning allows for safe exploration. If you carefully respect the natural unfolding with no influence, the organic outstretches on its own. Conserving and respecting the energy, you honor that space for the seed to sprout and grow.

Another way we can get blocked is when we think something is "good" with what we're creating; with an achievement, a relationship that's sailing, or anytime at all we think we've "arrived," something can happen to trip us up. Our creative process isn't always easy, but when we get hooked up, it's a relief. What we want more than anything is to believe it'll stay that way forever. In experiencing moments of freedom, there's a new inner bar to uphold and then we worry we won't be able to reach it again.

Once, I wrote an article that felt so good, so on point, that energy rushed through my body and I felt high. When I feel that kind of creative current, I know I'm connected to my open, present self. I thought, *This is the best thing*

I've ever written.

The next week when I had to write another article, I feared I couldn't make it as good as the last one. Not only did I fear it, my inner judge told me I definitely wouldn't be able to meet my new standard. And it was mostly because I had made the previous article too precious. My mind interpreted it as "my favorite" and "my best." *Well that was it, that's all I'm supposed to write in life, that's as good as it gets.*

As soon as I was able to identify my judgment, I gave myself permission to write whatever was present even if at first I thought it wasn't good in comparison. I didn't stop myself from returning to my computer and continuing. The more I wrote, the more I got back into the rhythm.

Good judgment can be as much of a block to our creative expression as bad judgment. We can have some good days where everything is great and then WHOA—something steps in that challenges us.

I've come to accept I will eventually lose momentum after being in the flow. After good experiences come, "bad" things will happen. After expansion, we always contract. That's how life goes. And that means nothing about us. The good news about feeling bad is that when we get thrown off course, there's an opportunity for us. With each letdown, our spirit strengthens by discovering the way out. "Down times" are our ally. Without *bad, good* wouldn't exist. We might as well make the most of it.

What wants to come through you is meant to come through because it's what you're supposed to learn about yourself through the experience of doing it. The awe and wonder that mysteriously reveals itself when you open to spontaneity and free expression enlightens your life's present moments. You can share it if you choose, but having time in the beginning can help you decipher what works and doesn't work for you.

To ignite and unleash, ask yourself what if:

- I could dare to jump?
- I could mess it up?
- I could continue to create along with the fear?
- I had permission to fail, screw up, or suck?
- I kept the fun in it?
- I didn't have to know what I'm doing, how I'm doing it, or how it will end up?

It takes everyone awhile to find footing. As you explore foreign lands and new territories, you have to be willing to get lost. Like traveling without a road map, the most fun of any trip is the unplanned places you stumble upon. Allowing others into your creative process too early can lead you astray from the unknown path that longs to enlighten you.

When a child first begins to draw, he doesn't understand dimensions or perspective. In a first attempt to draw a table, the legs may go vertically up, but over time the legs eventually come down. A parent understands this is a part of a child's development. They don't judge it or think something is wrong. They don't try to force the legs down. They know that over time, the child's table will stand upright. There is a space and time we need as we develop, even as adults.

Sometimes when you focus too intently on something, you can suck the breath out of it. Ruminating, getting caught in circular thinking, getting trapped inside your head, or trying to come to a conclusion around what you want or don't want can put you in a state of paralysis. Like when you're working so hard that you can't seem to get out of the stress-provoking loop. Sometimes you just need to go away for a weekend and let fresh air breathe new life into you. Giving yourself the time and space to create, you have more freedom to really explore what wants to be born from you.

How about:

- Going anywhere you're called to go?
- Creating for you and not for anyone else?
- Not having to have it all figured out?
- Allowing anything to happen?
- Remaining open to surprises?

It's all about you having permission to keep being a beginner. Over time, as you carry on you will become an expert. And even as an expert, you're constantly learning something new. So in actuality, you're always beginning—always being a beginner. When you decide you know all there is to know, that's when you stop improving.

You may get so overwhelmed that your indecisiveness could make you lose your drive or focus. It could cause you to disconnect from the innate passion that drives you. Even the smallest things can throw one off track. The point is to keep going until you trust the strength of your own foundation. It becomes more solid in the act of building it.

I wrote in Natalie's workshops in her style for three years. I held steadfast to her rule of "no comments" whenever I read out loud. I learned as I read; I could sense which part of the writing came alive and jumped off the page on my own. Rather than hear from others what they thought was good or interested them, I could sense when the writing engaged and when it didn't. In the reading of it, I could feel when I was truly present while writing, which parts touched an awakened place inside of me. I could feel in my body when I got distracted or bored or lost touch. Not good or bad writing, just getting words down first was the key.

And with life, the trick is to feel the energy. To sense when something feels right as we engage. When it doesn't, we know to shift course. When it's on point, we feel enlivened. Not good or bad choices—being aware of the energy first is the key. Who says that after we make a choice, we can't course correct? We always have choices when it comes to prioritizing.

I needed permission first to write with abandon. I needed my pen to take me to all kinds of nooks and crannies, to open unknown spaces, and ugly places, and emotional releases. I needed to get my pen moving without stopping. I filled forty spiral notebooks until I was ready to start writing a manuscript. I'd collected many gems that came from writing practice, gems I may not have discovered if I hadn't let myself write with unrestricted freedom.

In life, let yourself explore without comment. There isn't a right or wrong way to do it. Let go of needing it to be a finished, faultless "product." Focus only on the present moment and give yourself ample time to explore before sharing it.

WORKSHEET
Planting Your Seeds

The following worksheet can plant fresh ideas about what you want to start growing in your life. These seeds might even bloom bigger dreams! Keep them dear and see how they will sprout with a little water and sunshine.

1. I have a secret passion I've never told anybody, and that is:

_____

_____

2. My five favorite characters/stories from childhood and why I liked them:

1. _____

2. _____

3. _____

4. _____

5. _____

3. My top-five favorite books of all time and why I liked them:

1. _____

2. _____

3. _____

4. _____

5. _____

4. My top-five favorite songs and why I like them:

1. _____

2. _____

3. _____

4. _____

5. _____

5. My top-three favorite colors and why I like them:

1. _____

2. _____

3. _____

6. My top-three favorite animals and why I like them:

1. _____

2. _____

3. _____

7. My top-three favorite celebs / mentors / famous people and why like them:

1. _____

2. _____

3. _____

8. Write down in your journal the top themes and connections explored from these lists.

9. What does this insight reveal to you? Do they spark possible passions you could explore with inquiry? Do they lead to new ideas of how to engage your creativity? If so, write what comes forward for you.

10. If the world was about to end and you had a few precious moments to tell someone about what you really wanted to create in your life, what would you say? Write this in your journal.

11. Why are you the special one to birth this into the world? What innate gifts or talents do you have to offer? How might this be your true creative calling and connected to your life purpose? Write down the first thoughts that come to you.

Mistakes

> *Anyone who has never made a mistake has never tried anything new.*
>
> —Albert Einstein

Have you ever sat with a child and started to draw your own picture with their crayons? You're drawing a house with a tree, some flowers, and a sun, and all of a sudden, after going along quite nicely, you stop.

What's next? you think. But nothing comes, so you get up from the table while the child continues drawing.

Or you're coloring along quite happily and then *oops*, you think you've made a mistake. *Oh crap*, you think, and want to cover it up, erase it, start over again, or throw it away. The inner judge is back with a horrible disappointed frown.

The reason we stop like this is because of a desire for our creations to be perfect. In life, it's common to strive for perfection in our endeavors. We think, *If it's perfect, then I don't have to worry.* But in truth, it's actually the need to make it perfect that causes us to worry in the first place. Perfectionism is the chains, fence, cuffs, ropes, and straightjacket that squeezes the breath out of our lives.

Perfection is really just fear dressed in a beautifully pressed ball gown with a million meticulously sewn-on rhinestones. It's a setup for anxiety, since perfectionism forces us to micromanage and overcontrol. We dread that if we, or our plans, are not perfect, or we miss our step, everything will crumble and come crashing down.

We still strive for perfection, even though we find its pursuit can be nihilistic and annihilating. We teach our kids to color in between the lines. We obsess over immaculate spotlessness or creating the perfect idealized image. But one million people every year visit a small town in Italy called Pisa—not to see a beautifully built cathedral, but rather its tilting bell tower.

Imperfections are what color our lives. "Mistakes" can make originality and uniqueness and show our humanity. They're part of the process of creation. Imperfections and "mistakes" are actually *creativity's guides*: They take us on new adventures to traverse unknown, exciting territories. They ignite the unexpected that brings enchantment, beauty, and attraction into our daily lives. They bring allure and charm and provide a way to connect intimately.

Every single time I've painted an image that I thought was a mistake, I look back at the painting later on and that exact "imperfection" is what I love most about it. Though I thought I'd wanted it to be pristine, *creativity knew better*. Every time I'd hated something while I was painting because it looked ugly and not picture perfect, in the moments after I gave in and kept painting, I felt liberated. Imagination, intuition, and inventiveness allowed something unique that was unbeknownst to my rational, cautious mind to shine through—something perfection wouldn't have otherwise conceded.

Perfection makes us grasp for control, even though we know it's not ours to have. We feel the need to be more than human—to be Super Human at that. Perfection is just plain boring. What we need is to revel in the mistake-making freaks of nature we are. Otherwise, we aren't living this grand, gorgeous life creativity intended for us.

I'm fascinated when I look back at the paintings that I hated while painting them, the ones I wanted to rip up because they embarrassed me or looked ridiculous or "too dark," because oddly, these are the paintings that pop with the most energy. *I painted that?* I asked myself, forgetting what I'd channeled in my past. Even friends whom I've shown some of my paintings to will remark, "Who the hell did that?" It's not what they would expect from me and not what I expected either. But when I gave myself permission to explore everything I was feeling, my creativity took off, presenting an opportunity to tap into important parts of my being that my mind tried to tamp down.

A student in a painting workshop was a graphic designer for a living. I watched her the first day spend a lot of time choosing the colors for her painting before she even began painting, calculating and manipulating the entire finished product. She carefully placed every color she intended to paint with onto a palette. She sketched out the image she wanted to paint in detail and spent hours filling in the colors she'd already chosen, stepping back to look at the painting to make sure it was turning out exactly how she wanted it. If it wasn't how she wanted it, she obsessively fixed it.

I watched her grow tired and stressed, tied in knots as she painted. She stopped many times to take long breaks. She didn't seem to feel enlivened by the doing of it. It seemed like a job for her, even though I knew the reason she took the workshop was that she was looking to bring new life into her graphic design work. Deep inside, what she was really interested in was to break out of her usual creative routine and to open it up full swing.

Toward the end of the weekend workshop, I watched her feel safer and get out of her familiar patterns. She started to trust the process of creativity more and allowed herself to give in to its powerful call. As this happened, she was more energetic and elated to keep her brush moving, allowing more of what she hadn't planned or expected to enter her process.

What would happen if after drawing a pretty flower while coloring with a child, something crazy might enter into your picture? Like a big fire-breathing dragon that incinerated all the flowers? When a child draws a fire-breathing dragon, we don't think that there's something psychologically troubled with them. We're amazed they drew it. Allowing ourselves to explore what might be "bad" or "ugly" brings a certain kind of beauty with it. When we care more about meeting what is present inside of us and experiencing it without our preconceived notions of what it should be like, that freedom gives us instantaneous wild inspiration.

The beauty could be found in all our imperfections—the good, the bad, and even the ugly. That's the most powerful experience meant for us to receive. Just because it's not what we thought we wanted doesn't make it not good or right.

The more I'm willing to allow anything to arise, the less is hidden away from me. When I allow whatever wants to be seen to reveal itself, it's released, set free. But if I suppress it, it could be dangerous. In life, I could swallow my feelings and negatively impact my overall well-being, causing unnecessary stress and potentially affect my physical, emotional, mental, or spiritual health. When I avoid or deny what wants to arise in me, I could make self-harming choices from an unconscious or numbed-out place. But through the safety of creativity, when I rise up to meet the wondrous energy that is ready to depart from me, my preprogrammed fear no longer runs me.

Creative mistakes can be nature's blessings. They teach us courage, stretch us into greater expansiveness, and encourage us to trust. It took 177 years to build the Tower of Pisa and only ten years for it to start leaning, but it's now a beautiful, iconic world monument. An inventor named Richard Jones was designing a monitor tower for battleships; when one of the tension springs fell to the ground, the spring started bouncing around and eventually became the toy called Slinky. Sir Alexander Fleming, in his pursuit to cure diseases, threw away a petri dish only to discover that the mold from the bacteria formed contained penicillin. Ruth Wakefield, owner of the Toll House Inn, was making chocolate cookies and realized she was out of baker's chocolate. When she broke sweetened chocolate into pieces she expected them to melt, but the chunks didn't. A Canon engineer accidently rested an iron on his pen, which caused the pen to eject ink, and now we have the ink-jet printer. And an unknown chef in China was experimenting in the kitchen, combining charcoal, sulfur, and saltpeter, and now 2,000 years later the world celebrates with fireworks.

Sometimes we just don't get our preferences. Our inner critic demands a certain outcome when there could be many other interesting, innovative options we could explore or possibilities we didn't even know existed until they presented themselves to us. We try to take stake over our creation, ignoring nuance, and avoiding new routes that might just want to lead us to a new evolved place—something else that's more in alignment with our needs.

We've learned from experience that it's much more enjoyable when we aren't attached to the outcome. We know how much more we will get out of the whole experience when we simply relish the moments and let them unfold naturally. But sometimes, we can put a lot of pressure on ourselves, or others, for it to all come out the way we want. We can grip too hard to the point of suffocating the outcome—all because we long for it to be fabulous.

Far too often, we've found ourselves wanting certain things, and yet it doesn't always work out in the way we'd hoped. It's not a complete myth. We can create what we want. We can have more. We can with intention, clarity, and hard work achieve our goals.

It's important to self-validate and positively reinforce. To affirm our capabilities, to truly go after what we want, and to trust that we're not only meant to have it, we deserve it. Because we do! Yet, sometimes, no matter how much we would prefer something to turn out in a certain way, it doesn't. Then we can allow the creative current to guide us—whatever wants to can come forth in the way that creativity wants for us. It actually knows what's best. By staying open to what wants to come through us, creative energy reveals something we couldn't conceive of at first. We get to be surprised and curious about the experiences we couldn't have known that exist for us. Letting go gives us rock-our-socks-off Eureka moments. We learn not only to trust our life more but also to have less desire to control it. Maybe, just maybe . . . something greater than us might know more about what we *really* want.

Creativity has a higher cause, something beyond you that it wants you to experience, know, or see. A place it wants to lead you—somewhere new and expansive. This is more profound than what your limited mind can comprehend. Your creative calling gives you the gift of coming to understand your true priorities.

Have you ever wanted something so badly, didn't get it, and then realized there was actually another option that was more in alignment? Maybe you had a crush on someone who didn't have the same feelings for you. Later, when you started dating someone else, you could easily see how your first fleeting crush wasn't right for you at all.

Or perhaps you can think of a time when you listened to your intuition rather than to your rational mind. It turns out that you were being protected so you could end up someplace much better for you, both physically and emotionally.

What about a situation in which you were attached to a certain outcome and, when it didn't work out the way you wanted, you were actually more satisfied with an even better outcome?

Have you lost a job or watched a business fail only to realize later there was another job/career/acquisition that was better for you, waiting right around the corner?

This is how letting go of preference can support us to achieve even better results.

When we don't allow ourselves to let go and go with the flow, when we can't rest in the uncertainty and be curious about how things might unfold, it's like we're pushing away the aliveness and possibility that life wants for us.

All too often, our attachments to outcome can cause us to refuse creativity's benefits before we even begin. This is why attachments to our preferences can be the number-one creativity killer.

We set our true aspirations aside for another time and our attention goes on to something else, most likely something less meaningful, important, or significant. We give up way too fast, just when the energy is ready to inspire us. We snuff the light out before we give ourselves room to see what it illuminates. Plus, there's the stress that comes with trying to force our preferences out into the world. It wreaks havoc on our nervous systems. In its extreme, our need to will our desires into reality can make us become impulsive and obsessive.

My friend and past teacher, Don Miguel Ruiz, author of *The Four Agreements*, taught me this very powerful mantra. What if, when life isn't going the way we think it "should" or how others act isn't in alignment with our preferences, we say this to ourselves:

So what?
Who cares?
Big deal?
Why not?

There are no rules. We don't need to encumber others or ourselves to be, feel, or act a certain way. Our opportunity is to allow whatever is present, while also allowing something new that is ready to come out of us right now, ready to be born. Listening to our insides, the perspective shift comes from somewhere deep within when we are guided by the truth of our inherent intuition and its inherent wisdom.

What if it didn't matter if what you wanted to create was:

- Pretty or not?
- Good or not?
- Perfect or not?
- Right or not?
- Famous or not?
- The best thing you've ever done or not?
- Bad or not?
- Terrible or not?
- Ugly or not?
- Stupid or not?
- Ridiculous or not?
- A waste of time or not?
- Proved you were worthy or not?
- Loved or not?
- Seen or not?
- Acknowledged or not?

If *it really didn't matter or not*—why not continue? Why not see if something else might come that leads you to more brightness?

Permission is all that's needed. I guarantee you that if you meet whatever is fully present with self-awareness and open-minded receptivity, you'll continue into greatness. If it's "weird," meet it. If it's "dark," meet it. If it's "shit," meet it. If it's "hard," meet it. If it's interesting, meet it. If it's "scary," then definitely meet it. Don't indulge in what the mind might perceive as "negative"; just allow it. Even if it doesn't make sense and you have no idea what you're doing or where it's going—meet it. In fact, that's the perfect place for inspiration.

EXERCISE
Freedom from Control

What we have opportunity to create in order to live a freer, happier life is a wider perspective that ultimately offers more permission. Preference usually comes with a "should" attached. For example: *It should look like this. It should be like that. It should turn out like this. It should happen like that. It should work like this. He or she should act like this.*

1. Ask yourself: *What am I "should-ing"?*

2. Locate the "should."

3. Then, ask yourself: *What if it didn't matter if I/it/he/she was* _____

_____ *or not?*

Fill in the blank with the "should" and allow yourself to feel the openness, release, and expansion this offers. Stay curious. It takes practice with self-awareness to discover what your attachments and preferences are telling you. You don't need to encumber yourself by thinking that life should be a certain way, or you should feel a certain way, or that others should be a certain way. Listening to your insides, the perspective shift comes from somewhere deep within. That's what opens you up to your life's flow and freedom.

4. After asking this question, is there something you are interested in doing right now that offers you more freedom to explore? What draws you? What's your next step? Are you willing to take that next step right now? Write these answers in your journal.

Upsets

> *Develop a mind that is vast like the water, where experiences both pleasant and unpleasant can appear and disappear without conflict, struggle, or harm.*

—Buddha

Most of the time when we're stuck, down, or depressed, it's because we're feeling a way we don't want to feel and are trying to push it away. Negative emotions can take over and cripple us when we're facing adversity. We place a veil over our eyes so we don't have to feel what our mind deems as "bad." Yet, emotional experiences that arise are really offerings to show us what no longer serves us. Once upsets are cleared, they no longer have the power to run us. In truth, it's not the issues we think we're having that cause us problems. It's the way we react to the issues that does. Problems will always arise that cause emotional reactions. We can't avoid that. But our opportunity is to become aware of how we are reacting. We can uncover our feelings by allowing them to safely release without causing harm to others or ourselves.

The truth is that what we think are "problems" aren't really problems at all. And the reason for this is that most problems (if not all) are based on old memories. When we get upset it's because our mind registered thoughts in our subconscious that happened in the past, and we fall prey to them again in the present. A way through this is to understand the differences between emotions and feelings.

Emotions are thoughts put on a feeling. Feelings are simply an energy arising, ready to be released.

Feelings + Thought = Emotion

If we allow ourselves to feel what we're feeling without attaching a story or thought to it, the feeling can remain in its original state, a sensation that can easily pass. Any difficult emotion that arises is based on a stored memory the mind has carefully documented. It doesn't want us to be hurt again, so it shuts us down to protect us.

Whatever feelings arise, and the thoughts attached to them that create our emotions, are really offerings to show us what is ready to depart from us. That's the beauty of creation. Creativity is like Calgon rushing through a calcified pipe, taking with it whatever is in our way. It's more interested in how we can continue to grow and expand day by day.

When dealing with a problem, I tended to say, "*Oh NO*" and closed up and shut down, only to find that a relatively short time later I would say, "*WHEW— Well, thank God that's over.*" It does pass . . . but what made it so painful or difficult while it was happening was that I believed things that were said about me or I was told that, for some reason, I still wanted to hold on to. What I most wanted was for a not-enoughness to be enough, an unlovability to be loved, a wrong to be righted, or the truth that I was not broken.

Once we understand that the thoughts attached to our feelings are just lies and that we shouldn't let them run us, we can then focus simply on allowing the feeling to gently release. Feelings on their own can move away quickly like a cloud moving across a sky, leaving us with spaciousness. Our emotions ask us to feel so we can go to the next level in ourselves. We may not want to take that risk, but when we expose ourselves to our vulnerabilities, we are actually strengthened. Now we can create more of what we really want in our life and relationships.

There really are only four basic feelings. Once you drop the thoughts attached to them, you can use them to help guide you much more easily:

1. Anger
2. Fear
3. Sadness
4. Joy/Love

Underneath your anger is fear. Under fear is sadness. And under sadness is where your joy and loving lies. When you can pinpoint which feeling you feel on this continuum, you can then uncover the feeling underneath. If you're angry, for certain there is fear. When you locate the fear, you will find a tender place inside that usually has tears or grief associated with it, many times if not most times from your past. Once the tears are allowed to be present, you will return to the permeating love that always exists inside your whole being.

When a man I was in a close, intimate relationship with couldn't meet my needs, my initial impulse was to be angry, even enraged. Although it was only a made-up story that I wasn't worthy of being loved, I'd still fight against the injustice when he pushed me away, cheated, lied, or cut off without reasoning. I'd blame him for not giving me what I wanted, even though it was me who was repeating the patterns of choosing unavailable men. I'd give him a mouthful of everything I thought was wrong with him, criticizing, analyzing, and judging him. When in truth, it was me who believed there was something wrong with me, and that made me unavailable to loving my own self fully. It was so much easier for me to make it about someone else, rather than my own reflection.

Usually when we're angry, we're blaming someone else or something external for our upset. It's important to become aware of what we're putting on someone else, and examine how we're giving them power over our own emotions and peace of mind. Any anger, reactions, or complaints are our responsibility—not the person who triggers us. Whatever they do or don't do is not our business.

Our inner experience projects like a movie projector onto a screen. That movie is our creation. Everything we think, see, and feel comes from within us, and what we see in another person reflects back to us so we can see ourselves. Freud called this projection, and it's an important psychological principle to understand. Our interactions with the people we encounter are the greatest ways to see what is unresolved within us. Our relationships are our greatest teachers because they mirror what is hidden in our unconscious. If we understand this principle and how it works, our relationships can be transformed. There's a purpose the mirror of the other has been brought to us so that we can learn about what's unresolved within us.

When triggered by someone you're in relationship with, identify the upset and then look into the mirror.

Ask, is there:

- A part of me that's like that?
- A way I act like that?
- A way I feel like that?

- A way I treat myself like that?
- A way I've treated someone else like that?
- A way I'm judging myself like I feel judged?
- A way I'm judging them or someone else in the same way I feel they're judging me?
- A story from my past that this reminds me of that has opportunity to be reframed and updated?

For example, let's say I was angry with my partner for not loving me in the way I wanted, and I felt rejected. I could then ask myself, "Is there a part of me that feels unlovable or unworthy of love? Do I love myself in the way I want to be loved? Am I rejecting a part of myself? Is this person treating me how I'm treating myself? Am I rejecting him or rejecting others in the same way or in another way, causing another to feel similarly to how I feel?" These questions could lead me into taking more responsibility for my situation.

Or let's say you feel upset because someone is criticizing you and there's nothing you can do to please them. Nothing is ever enough. You could ask yourself, "Am I unnecessarily hard and critical of myself or other people? Do I put unfair expectations on myself? Is there a story that happened in my past that made me buy into the belief that I'm not enough?"

When this is shifted in you, you won't be triggered by what someone else does or does not do. You won't take it personally. You can make choices from a compassionate place, not from a place of blame or victim but from a place of love and self-loving. The mirror of relationships teaches you how to be your best self, living more peacefully.

Coming to understand your reactions and using them as your teacher makes difficult, threatening situations much easier. You learn to become an observer so that you can catch yourself quicker in the act. Your negative reactions may never go away, but with awareness you can begin to make changes and course correct more quickly. Self-awareness with kindness is the primary key to your greatest reconciliation.

WORKSHEET
Working through an Upset with Another Person

1. Fill in the blanks:

I am upset with _____ because _____

_____

_____

2. Is there something you are trying to avoid seeing in yourself?
   What might that be?

_____

_____

3. Is there a way you are acting this way with this person, another person,
   or yourself?

_____

_____

4. Ask yourself, *What am I willing to take responsibility for?* Write down options
   for what you are willing to take responsibility for in regard to this person
   being your mirror. Then, laser to the core and fill in the blanks:

I am willing to take responsibility for _____.

_____

_____

_____

_____

5. Ask yourself, *What can I do to enforce a positive change?* Explore options for what you're willing to do in a new way to actualize change. Perhaps it's an apology. Perhaps you are willing to share what your participation is in the situation. Perhaps you could offer an act of heartfelt generosity to the other.

I am willing to actualize change by

_____

_____

6. How could you validate and acknowledge the other person for their feelings? How might you offer love, appreciation, compassion, and understanding?

_____

_____

· ·

The Buddhist monk Pema Chodron teaches a cool metaphor in regard to how to handle upsets. Let's pretend you're holding your hand in a fist. And let's say this fist represents your bottled-up feelings that are being expressed through anger, frustration, irritation, or impatience. Now imagine you took your other hand and gently patted the hand that's in the fist. The fist may not like that, so it punches the palm of the other hand. Your free hand continues to lovingly pat your fist, which becomes defensive and hits up against your open hand again. But after the free hand keeps gently patting the fist for a while, the fist eventually softens. It does let go. And the upset, which created the fist's tension in the first place, dissipates. Simply send any anger you feel patience, kindness, and tenderness, because what's underneath the bottled-up feeling is a need for loving attention.

As humans we are conditioned not to cry. We don't want to be judged as "too emotional." We want to stand firmly in regard to our careers and our families and have a social impact. We won't admit our fears. It can be hard to express vulnerability. We take on a lot. We feel like we have to keep it together because of our daily responsibilities. Sometimes we get angry rather than allow ourselves to touch the soft, fragile places we feel inside. We suppress it with all kinds of things like work, food, overanalysis, and stress. But impatience, irritation, and frustration are more ways that we cover up what's really going on. The trick is not to justify our feelings before "feeling" them. Justifying our reactions comes from judgment, not our heart center. And it's the heart that the fist most resists.

Nine times out of ten, I discover after giving my emotions a little "pat," perhaps along with a simple cry, the pressure gets released. I'm back at peace, feeling relieved.

What are you feeling underneath the story of your upset? Give yourself permission to embrace it, softly. What you feel doesn't have to be so bad. It passes quickly with a gentle touch, a gentle hand. Even with great trauma, losses, death, the greatest injustices, betrayal, received abuse, or neglect, our opportunity is to find our own tender loving for ourselves. In fact, it's even more crucial in our most-troublesome moments. Our mind knows how harming it was, so it blocks us from a potential rewounding. All our defenses go up. But, like a warrior, it takes courage, strength, bravery, and fortitude to heal. It also takes humility. A true warrior knows not to go to extremes or react off-handedly, but to practice restraint. She doesn't fight for destruction but for love.

In those relationships with men, I was always surprised to find that my anger was trying to protect me from having to feel the terror of being abandoned again. My mind only wanted information it could control, but becoming aware of my fear was the most important next step. When I felt not wanted fully by a man, it triggered the most fragile stored feelings of the infant inside me who was rejected. The threat of the separation opened my primal adoption wound. I learned that what I needed most was to feel the grief of my genesis and let go with a deep release. Allowing myself to experience these infantile feelings, I could find my own beating heart again. I could lay Baby Lynn on my own chest, what I didn't receive from my biological mother at birth, and give her the warmth and nurturance she needed. Each time I returned to my loving, I closed the gap of separation, and my innate ability to love myself strengthened. If I loved myself above everything else, what others did or didn't do needn't be taken so personally, and I'd choose differently.

It took me years to heal, unpack, and uncover these patterns. But we have to start somewhere. We can't move beyond blockages until we're willing to feel our feelings to create what we really want. If we want love, we have to feel the fear under our anger and the sadness covering our ability to have it. If we want peace and happiness, we have to feel the feelings in the way of our fulfillment. Feeling our feelings safely and gaining the trust to allow them is a process that takes practice. But it really can be very simple and not a huge psychological examination. For example, I was angry I wasn't getting the love I wanted. I was afraid of losing someone I loved. I felt sadness around the grief of it. And when felt, I could come back home to myself.

EXERCISE
Overcoming Anger Quickly

1. When the defense mechanism of anger rears itself, ask yourself: *What am I really angry about?* Give that anger a voice in a safe place alone or with someone you trust.

2. Then try to narrow down whatever story you are telling yourself to a simple sentence or two, identifying the core of the upset. This helps brings clarity.

3. Look for the fear. Ask yourself: *What am I really scared of?* And give whatever arises a voice rather than suppressing it.

4. Then ask yourself: *Could I be vulnerable and allow tears if they are here to come?*

5. Touch your heart and see where your loving lies. How might you love another or yourself better? What gratitude could you summon to embrace the fullest amount of love available for you? Place your hand on your heart and close your eyes. Then speak out loud what your heart most needs to express from a loving place of compassion and appreciation.

Fear

I remember, in my twenties, one of my painting teachers, Carol Levow, carefully moseyed across from the corner of the studio, with hands gently resting inside her apron's pockets to check in with me. Carol was grounded and earthy, lived in Northern California, and was like a big sister to me. She had studied with Michele for many years to become a teacher. She was sometimes softer than Michele, less penetrating, and more patient with me. Usually, I was happy she was coming over, trusting she'd always take me to another deeper level in myself. But when I was most anxious and afraid of what was arising in me as I painted, I'd feel her coming closer, and tense up. This was one of those times.

Don't mess with me, I thought. Even though I knew Carol only wanted to help me unleash.

This day happened at a two-week painting workshop in Taos, which I'd never forget. I was painting along, but when Carol began moving toward me, suddenly I was starving, obsessed with eating a Snickers bar. A Snickers was not my usual indulgence. I've had less than a handful of Snickers in my entire life. But that day, I wanted a Snickers bar more than anything else. I was so fixed on this candy craving that when Carol walked up to chat about my painting process, I quickly rushed off.

"I'll be a back in a second," I told her and hightailed it into my Jeep to go to the local convenience store.

Upon returning, I ripped the paper off the supersize bar with my teeth and gnawed at chocolate-covered peanuts, nougat, and caramel, holding out an extra Snicker to Carol as a peace offering.

I was closed off to her assistance and was stuffing my face, and all Carol could do was laugh back at me. It was funny, even though I took that Snickers bar *very* seriously.

All I wanted, more than anything else, was to avoid what was being asked of me to feel underneath my fear. Even though the outcome could have been something potentially mind blowing and life changing.

"I'm eating," I said to her as she stepped closer to me. "Want some?"

Carol smiled, noting my resistance with a sideways glance, and moved back into the corner.

That wasn't the only time I met up with my own inscrutable resistance in those painting workshops. Once, I rolled into a ball on the floor underneath my painting and sobbed.

Carol came over with hands in pockets, feet together, and leaned over me. "What's going on here?" she said gingerly.

We both knew if I kept painting I would have a gentler way through, but the drama my fears were creating paralyzed me.

Another time I was having a panic attack, spinning out, flailing my hands, holding the brush, and trying to convince Carol that whatever she was offering to help me get out of my block was ridiculously stupid.

"May I have your brush?" she asked, as if I was waiving a weapon in my hand. "Come stand with me," she said. She stood next to me in front of the painting and delicately asked, "What's the next color you would choose?"

Like a small child, I walked to the table to get some light blue, wiping a tear.

I can have a strong, sometimes tough personality, and gratefully, there have been several people in my life who've known how to deal with me. Carol kept me safe with her nurturing, comforting, big-sister qualities. No matter what I was going through, I knew she was right around the corner, with her hands in her apron, sweetly ready and willing to assist whenever I was resistant.

Carol challenged me—but with *love*. I'm eternally grateful for having such a wonderfully compassionate and understanding friend there for me, even throughout all my fearful bucking up. Partly because of her, I learned how to be on my own with my feelings and allow them to safely rise up and out. Eventually, outside the painting workshops and in my own life, I learned how to stand grounded and confident with my own hands in my own pockets.

If we don't touch our vulnerability, our fear can turn into debilitating anxiety. As soon as we feel our fear, our mind judges it as wrong. Then we become more anxious because our mind judges us for judging it all as wrong. Then it can turn into panic because the mind judges us for judging it, for judging it all as wrong. This judging upon judging is what makes our fear carry us away. All the expectations, inner/societal/cultural pressures, and beliefs that have informed us that our fear is wrong wrap it all up into one giant weight that crushes us. We're not supposed to feel afraid of *anything*, let alone cry when none of it makes sense to us.

The only way out is to appreciate and value our fear. We're supposed to feel fear. Not only are we supposed to, we need it, simply because it's a messenger telling us something *is* wrong, and it's crucial we hear it. We may be doing too much and need to slow down, or we're not in a supportive place and need to make changes immediately. The present moment may be informing us of something that's ready to be healed from our past, or we want to force a change in another or ourselves and need to take a step back. In reality, there's a threat to our physical, mental, emotional, or spiritual health. But feeling vulnerability is scary because we think it's in that exact place we will be hurt. So our mind grips, or locks down, or numbs us out, or acts out, or puts up defenses, or makes us want to run away. It thinks vulnerability means insecurity, and that's a lie. It shames our most tender, loving selves.

After I gently allow my tears to release, the anxiety subsides. Many times, I don't know why I feel the need to cry. It just doesn't seem to match the trigger. *Aren't I stronger? Aren't I more capable? Why am I such a baby?* Ah, but there's my inner judge again, shaming me. It's not only okay; it's essential to give attention to the small, childlike, sensitive parts of myself. Anyone who told us it's not okay to cry was probably the one who needed it most. It's vital to empty our cup when it has become too full. It could save our life.

There was a crucial lesson that reemerged fifteen years later, when I was overwhelmed by emotion the week after my mother had passed away. In my haze of grief and alone, painting was the one place I knew I could release. It wouldn't matter what I painted; it was for me, my needs, and nothing else. A skeleton emerged whose stomach was full of skeletons and dark-red blood falling from its eyes. Skeletal hands reached for the skeleton. Death had taken its hold. I was ripped open inside. My mother had died.

Even though the painting came pouring out of me, I still couldn't help but think, *Whoa, this is dark. Whoa, this is heavy.* Certainly, I would never let anyone see it. If I did, what would they think of me? I feared they would think I was a dark and troubled person. But in that moment, I was in such despair—how someone perceived me mattered less than just having a place to deal.

When I finished, I put the painting underneath my bed with all of my past paintings, stacked in narrow boxes. I left it there for a few months. One day, I pulled it out and was astonished. The painting that took me so emotionally into the depth of death was *so alive*. A painting that initially brought up so much judgment about what it meant about me was now something I saw as amazingly free—scary, ugly skeletons and all.

What if:

- You could let yourself be bad—very bad, but consciously not destructively?

- You safely let loose, went too far, over the top, or didn't hold back?

- The "nutty person" could come into the room and feel the feeling for you? Could that side of you give you more permission to feel what you're feeling?

- You accepted what arose in you with care but without worry?

- Something wild, risky, or daring could take you to a new place inside yourself?

These questions can be very freeing, especially when we feel fear. But we also have to be careful. This isn't about getting ourselves into a mood when we want to harm others or ourselves, or tear something up, or react by destroying whatever's in front of us.

Once, I was writing in my journal and I got so sick of what I was writing that I threw my journal out in the trash. Once, when I was painting, I disliked an image so much that I used big globs of black paint to cover it up. Once, after gaining weight, I got so upset that I no longer fit into my clothes—I gave them all away. And once, I was angry and sad and poured myself some wine and then said, *screw it*, and poured some more.

For an instant, I felt relief. It felt really great in the moment. But soon after, I missed the journal that held within its pages potential material. When I painted over my artwork, I felt like a failure. I didn't want to continue, and it took some time for that interest to come back. I lost the weight, eventually, and really wished I had my favorite good-money-spent outfits that I felt great wearing. And of course, after all the wine, I had one hell of a hangover.

Obviously, something powerful arose inside of me when I wanted to throw my journal away. I covered up a feeling because it just seemed easier to rid myself of it. Rather than keeping my pen moving across the page, I may have had a release that was far more healing. Plus, it may have given me fresh insight, something undiscovered and revealing.

The time and attention I put into the specific detail in my painting before I covered it up came from presence and integrity. Once I slathered it with black paint, it was like burying myself. There were other ways to move through the intensity of what I was experiencing. If I stayed present to what I was feeling, I could have met it with care, respect, and attention. Continuing to paint could have given me new awake energy rather than bitterness or shame.

Rather than bag up my clothes and give them away, I may have found myself sitting on the floor in my closet, having a gentle cry. The tears may have informed me why I was eating more than I wanted to. They may even have motivated me to start eating healthily.

And obviously, drinking was self-harming. Too often, when I wanted to destroy something, I ended up hurting myself.

When we let ourselves feel what we're feeling, we gain power and self-esteem. We build a stronger, internal infrastructure. It's a lie that if we block out, deny, push away, or anesthetize what arises for us, we'll feel better. We get too caught up in what our feelings mean. Feelings are like a powerful current of water that will break the dam of suppression eventually. But instead of a dam, what breaks is our courage, morale, and self-trust.

If you feel a sense of hopelessness or suicide ideation or have difficulty coping, please seek medical attention or a skilled, trained counselor in your area. Find support groups. Do not isolate. You never, ever have to do this alone, and you shouldn't.

Destruction never benefits you or feels good in the end. Instead, it destabilizes you. Know that you're safe to allow your feelings to pass when felt with compassion. Trust that they're there to guide you because something new is ready to be liberated.

I've come to understand that when I hit my biggest emotions, there's something right around the corner ready to make new life for me. The moments when huge feelings arise, another level of greatness lies right on the other side. Creativity wants this for me. It wants me to release what no longer serves so that I can create my dreams.

Too often, we get so wrapped up in an emotion we don't know how to get simple. We overdramatize. We fall victim. When a negative thought attached to a feeling arises, drop it. Set it aside. Don't allow it to hold power over your freedom. Locate one of the five feelings—anger, fear, sadness, joy, and loving— and lean into them to strengthen. Feel the feeling kindly and with loving permission. It's amazing how quickly the sensation passes when we love it.

Emergency Tools
When Anxiety Gets the Best of You

1. **Ground:** To find your sense of security, anchor yourself and establish roots into the earth. Take care of your physical needs. Get into your body fully. Exercise. Do yoga. Dance. Stay away from sugar, caffeine, alcohol, and other stimulants. Sit on the ground next to a tree or lie on your back on the grass. Imagine a wide cord from your pelvis consciously rooting yourself into the core of the Earth. Walk slowly while breathing deeply and focus on feeling the bottoms of your feet, heel to toe. Drink a glass of water and sense it hydrating your whole body. Or get into a bath. These will all help you get grounded.

2. **Center:** When you feel like things are spinning out of control, the most important thing you need to do is connect to your own center. Draw your energy in. Rather than depend on others, give yourself the support, the love, the attention, the rest, the companionship, the kindness, and the understanding you need right now. Speak to your Higher Self, the All-Knowing, omnipotent wise one inside you who has vision, direction, and purpose and knows the truth of your circumstance.

   Ask your Higher Self: *What is for my highest good right now?*

   As if you were writing a scene in a play, write out a dialogue between the two of you. Ask your Higher Self whatever questions are necessary to feel like you have received the extra support you need.

3. **If you don't want to cry in public:** Roll your eyes in a big circle in one direction and then the other direction. It cuts at the tear ducts and will stop tears immediately.

4. **If you're having a panic attack:** Grab a less-than-full water bottle and toss it from one hand to the next. Focus on the water in the bottle as it moves between your hands. This will help balance out your brain synapses.

5. **Find laughter:** Last, and it may seem trite, if you can't tap into the tears under the fears, just *laugh*. Find any way you can to keep it light and not take it so seriously. Amusement can be your best friend in these circumstances and shift the energy fast.

Showing Up

One Saturday morning, shortly after my mother passed, my dog, Lita, had died, and Shlomi had moved out, my good friend Angela knew what I was going through and invited me to go with her to the Huntington Gardens in Pasadena. I had been planning to spend my day holing up on the couch to watch Netflix and eat pizza, but I couldn't say no to a day with Angela.

I'd been to the gardens many times, but somehow on this occasion "smelling the roses" took on a whole new meaning. We actually *did* smell the roses, pressing large, soft handfuls of petals to our faces (in fact, the essence of rose is said to combat depression), and just for the fun of it, we hugged this beautiful Ombrà tree from Argentina before laying a blanket on vibrant green grass.

It was the end of February in Southern California, and the sun was shining. I felt so grateful and blessed to be in warm weather in the middle of winter. We watched children play. We talked about our lives, lost loves, past travels, and friends we had in common, and listened to a guided meditation on genuine happiness. An elderly couple sat near us on a bench. A young man took pictures of his girlfriend doing a cartwheel across the lawn. The sun kept shining.

Rather than shutting down, Angela helped me get out of the house. I was so happy I said yes when my usual MO at that time of mourning was to say no. I was so pleased I showed up for a day strolling in the sun with my friend whom I loved. I came home refreshed after a Saturday afternoon well spent. I had newfound energy. I wanted to write. Paint. Be creative.

Our creative life force is something we can find in any moment—when we're connected with another person intimately, coming close with nature, or finding a new perspective that's different. Sometimes, when feeling low, we simply need to stretch out of our comfort zone and look for the beauty in our surroundings, the kind that gives us simple joy and pleasure.

When I feel connected to friends, community, my creativity, or my artistic expression, something that makes me feel alive, gives me energy, or turns me on, I don't care about anything else. My normal complaints don't matter. I'm connected to something much bigger, a current that carries me.

Heartfelt connection could come from a lunch with stimulating conversation, laughter, and love. Or being part of a community event where you feel of service to the larger whole. It could also come from clipping a new recipe and cooking a beautiful meal, starting a new knitting project of a sweater made of soft wool, or a holiday spent with your family. Whatever the "thing" is that gives you moments of sustained, present connection fulfills you in the doing of it. You're *there*, taken away by it, *becoming*. Time passes without your realizing. You don't want it to end—in a deep romance with the energy that connection embodies.

I could have closed the blinds and watched back-to-back Netflix episodes, choosing to stay in sludge. Or stare at the painting on my wall rather than pick up the brush. But I also knew I was sick of the tenth season of *Dexter*, and if I didn't give myself permission to show up for something, I'd go crazy.

In an interview Oprah had with Lady Gaga, Gaga said that in the past, when she was younger, she'd hole herself up in a hotel room and commit all kinds of debauchery, waiting to find her next spark of creative inspiration. Like most artists, she feared it wouldn't come. But ultimately it would, and then she'd throw herself into her work again. Obviously, this isn't the most supportive way to deal with uncertainty. But what makes it challenging is that we think there's something wrong with us for experiencing the discomfort. We all have those days where we question everything, where we want to retreat and hide out. And those days are important. We need to find space from the normal stresses of daily life, pull our energy in, and regenerate. In fact, as a Western culture we have opportunity to give ourselves permission to have days of restoration far more often. But we can also find ourselves falling into a stuck pattern, when what we have opportunity to do is to get out of isolation and connect with something that enlivens us.

A Quick Enlivening Exercise

1. Write out a list of ten simple things that you love, that when you experience them, you feel a moment of connection, a heart pull, or a simple feeling of everything being all right for the moment. For me it could be curling up on my couch with my organic cotton blanket, reading a good page-turner, or sitting outside in the sunshine with my journal, or taking a drive with my windows down and the music blaring. What are these simple things for you?

1. _____

2. _____

3. _____

4. _____

5. _____

6. _____

7. _____

8. _____

9. _____

10. _____

2. Keep this list close when you're having a down day and wondering how to get out of it. It's truly the simple natural things that give us pleasure. They offer love, gratitude, and appreciation.

3. State out loud what you appreciate right now in your life. When you step into the energy of appreciation, your energy ignites. There is also opportunity to not only state what you appreciate but also to elaborate on *why*. This takes the context of "reward" to a much-deeper level. Do it right now and then try it out each night before going to bed or in the morning right when you awaken. It closes the day nicely and helps to bring joy and light to your day.

Another way to get out of feelings of being stuck or lethargy, a time when you're overcome with grief or depression, and even the smallest task is difficult to do, is to put your attention on something else.

You know those things you've been putting off for a while? That thing you just don't want to get to, but your instincts are telling you that you should? You don't want to make the time for it, telling yourself you'll get to it eventually? Like fixing a shelf, updating your resume, putting together a scrapbook, filling some papers, or cleaning out the garage? There's an exercise class you've wanted to take, phone calls to catch up on, the creative project you'd love to do but you can't find the time or space. Choose *one* task to do. Keep it simple. Don't make it a huge overwhelming task, but switch up your energy by taking a step toward action. By doing it, you will get your energy moving again, and you will forget what you felt like before when it's all over. It'll totally shift your mood.

Questions to ask during these times:

- What's the easiest thing I can do in this moment?
- What's the path of least resistance?
- What are the simplest steps I can take right now?

When you're resisting doing that thing you know you want to do, that thing you know that *if* you do, you will feel great about yourself after doing it, ask yourself what is the easiest first step. It could be simply to pick up the phone and make one call. Take the stairs to the basement and open one box. Scratch the *easiest* to-do task off your list, like that dry cleaning that hasn't been picked up for a week. Get outside and take a twenty-minute walk. The point is to start somewhere. Somewhere easy.

Usually, that something that pulls on you is so happy to have your attention that it makes you elated for just showing up. It gives you a giant hug. Even if it feels like drudgery at first, somehow one step awakens you. Your energy comes alive again, and you feel good about yourself in the simple act of *accomplishing*. As you continue to take action steps, that gratified feeling accumulates, continuing to increase your energy.

I keep a painting up on my wall at all times. Whenever I have a moment, even on my busiest days, I can walk by, pick up a brush, and do something small on the painting just for a few minutes. Collected minutes add up, and I'm always surprised when a painting is finished before I even realize I've been completing it in increments. Just a few minutes a day accumulates results. Obviously, if we keep putting it off for a later date, it never happens. We think we need to devote all our time and energy to it, and that's just not the case. It's amazing what we can accomplish in just one minute.

If there's something we're resisting, there's a reason why we're resisting it. It's deeper than what it seems, something we're avoiding, usually because of underlying feelings. But as soon as we do it, it does this marvelous thing—*it smiles back at us.*

But what if you keep getting distracted? An increasingly big issue in our internet-connected world.

Let's say I have a project that I scheduled time out for today. And I've known for a week that this was the day. But as soon as I sit down to start, the phone rings, and I've got to take the call. Next thing I know, I receive a Facebook notification. So I log in to check out how many people liked an update I posted. Then I notice I'm thirsty, so I go get myself an iced herbal tea. I stretch and realize I'm feeling stiff, so I do some quick yoga. After I cool off on the sofa, I catch up on a few minutes of *Housewives* on Bravo. Before I know it, it's lunchtime, so I head to the kitchen . . .

It's not my fault. Not really. It's what my mind does, a way of protecting me from having to meet discomfort.

But why do we get so uncomfortable? Because we think we have to get the whole thing done. The pressure is on. We don't think about just starting from where we are, in the present moment, taking one small step. Nope. We think about all the steps it's going to take to finish the project. We count the hours or weeks in our heads that it's going to take to complete it. We look into the future, fearing all that we have to do to accomplish, and we feel understandably overwhelmed.

We simply don't want to do it because it brings up fears in us. For instance, fear of success, of being judged, rejection, the stretch it's asking of us, or anything else we might be afraid of. But if we start where we are, and simply begin, we might actually discover our fear is lying to us.

In the *The War of Art*, Steven Pressfield talks about what it takes to be a warrior as an artist. His suggestion is to show up under all circumstances every day and treat it like a job. It not only generates commitment but also sets a foundation to keep producing, even if it's not a particularly "good" writing day. Stephen King says in his book *On Writing* that he does the same thing. Natalie Goldberg encourages her students to schedule time each week. Julia Cameron, author of *The Artists Way*, suggests "morning pages" each day. Showing up brings self-esteem and also strengthens our productivity muscles. But if we want the rewards of productivity, we have to first give ourselves permission.

Since I know sometimes my fear can get in my way, I have a rule: If it's writing I'm meant to do, I head straight for my keyboard and I don't let myself touch anything else. I put my fingers on the keys and start typing. I don't let myself stop. I don't let anything interrupt me. I barely even let myself pee. And if what I write is crap, then it's crap. But at least I'm writing. And you know what? Even if I don't finish what I wanted to do, I feel *good* because I showed up. I took action. I made something happen. I tackle this with anything I have the opportunity to do.

Over time, if we keep showing up, it'll eventually get done. What is needed at this time is simple permission. And sometimes we just need someone to take our hand and give the permission for us.

My good friend Esther, who's a screenwriter, called me one day full of anxiety.

"I don't know where I am, what to do, and I scheduled time to write today, but I just don't want to do it. Everything I wrote yesterday was terrible. I thought I knew where the arc of my story was going. I think I'm going to go get a manicure instead," she told me.

"Where are you right now?" I asked her.

"At my desk."

"Good. Put your fingers on the keyboard and write," I said.

"That's all I need to do?"

"Yes. Don't stop your fingers from typing. Call me after two hours."

Two days later she texted me, "I finished my first draft. Woo hoo!"

That's all we need, really, as the artists of our lives—a little encouragement, a gentle hand of permission. Once we acknowledge what wants to be seen, creativity beams down upon us because it's so relieved. When we put our attention on what we want, it opens up all kinds of new possibilities.

Esther called me again on another day, when she got stuck on her second draft of her screenplay. She was ready and willing to write, but the writing wasn't coming. She explained she was starting the next draft on the first scene.

Our minds are linear. We think that when we sit down to begin working on a project, we should start at the beginning, continue through the middle, and then go on to the end.

"Is there a part of the story that draws you the most?" I asked.

"Well, I've been thinking about this one character, and I'd like her to be different. There's this one scene where she's acting this way and I want her to act another."

"Start there," I told her.

"Really? Shouldn't I start the second draft from the beginning?"

"Isn't that scene the place that has the most energy?"

"Yes!" she admitted.

When we're in tune, we feel a yes! Our intuition knows. It tells us we've arrived at the right place, even if our mind questions it. Our body sighs with relief, and that helps clarify our next action. It may not be the answer we thought it would be, but with a little permission we almost never hesitate to answer immediately.

Another way we can get blocked is when we make what we want to create too "special." Like a New Year's Eve on the town, or a Valentine's romantic dinner, or our wedding night, or that birthday cake we're baking. We want it to be beautiful. We want it to be lovely. We want it to be outstanding. And sometimes it is. Sometimes it all works out the way we planned and foresaw. And sometimes it doesn't. And we're grown up enough to know that that's how life works out even if we feel disappointed.

When we want to produce something but are so caught up in it having to be significant, special, or important, we're controlling it. Control takes us out of spontaneity and creative freedom. The tension itself can ruin the experience or add unnecessary stress.

If I sit down to write with the self-imposed expectation to write something amazing, I may find myself staring at a blank screen. I lose the freedom to write junk, to make shit—it takes me out of the current of creativity. When painting, I may see an image in my mind that I want to re-create on paper, but when I try to paint it, it doesn't come out exactly like a Mind-Xerox machine. Feeling let down, I might put my brush down too, blocking any spontaneous expression.

If we think we must be special, or seen as special, or do that *one* thing that no one has *ever* done, then we can get stifled.

What if:

- You could let go of thinking life should be a certain way to be truly free?

- Whatever you are doing didn't have to be your best, and you could relax, enjoying your time with it?

- It didn't have to blow your socks off?

- No one liked it?

- You didn't worry about the results?

- You didn't make a big deal about it?

- You didn't take it too seriously but still went about it mindfully?

Phew! Now we're off the hook. Space opens up with permission. We're flowing again. The grasp of holding something so dear, so tight, so close . . . loosens and opens. Instead of getting caught in the ego of "specialness," we get to *just be real*. We're unimpeded to allow *anything* to happen. And whatever does happen, we don't have to take it personally. It doesn't say anything about us.

Exercise
Showing Up

1. **Decide what it is that you want to create this week for yourself**. It could be anything. More self-care. A new creative activity. More love in your relationship. Whatever you want. Write down in your journal your plan and date for when you want to start, like tomorrow, or within a reasonable time frame.

2. **The night after your planned date, review what you promised yourself**. Did you do it? If you didn't do it, why? In what way could you give yourself more permission to begin?

3. **Continue to do this every day for a week**. Did you continue to show up? How might you continue every day to give yourself even more permission?

4. **Each day, if you followed through, acknowledge yourself by writing out how it felt for you**. We rarely take the time to acknowledge ourselves when we accomplish something, and it's super important in raising our esteem, energy, and frequency. What do you appreciate about your experience? How does showing up bring lightness and joy to you?

11

Meaning

Two years after my Mom died, the overwhelming grief had passed. I became used to not having her at the table at our family holidays, or talking to her on the phone every other day, or holding her soft, white, freckled hand. But this one quiet Saturday night when I was alone at home, my grief welled up out of nowhere. I ached from missing her. I thought I shouldn't feel that way. After all, it had been two years. I'd indulged in my grief long enough, and I thought if I spent any more time feeling those feelings, it would mean that I was emotionally frozen. My inner judge told me to grow up, that I was an adult now, and I needed to care for myself. I thought this was a horrible way to be spending my time on a Saturday night, and instead I should go out, meet friends, or be on a date.

But I couldn't stop thinking of her. I found myself talking to her out loud. *Mom, could you come back for just a second? I forgot who you were.*

I remembered I had a file of mail she had sent me over the years: birthday cards, thank-you notes, loving reminders when I was homesick after I'd moved from home to Los Angeles for college. She crafted letters with her stunning handwriting. I can't see her unique penmanship and not feel close to her. I took out the file and opened each card, reading every thing she wrote to me over the course of my adult life. She was *there*, speaking to me, and I cried deeply for some time. But rather than it feeling like overwhelming grief, I felt overwhelming love. My heart swelled. It was too hard during those last two years to look at those letters. I kept them filed away. But that Saturday night, two years later, I felt ready. I read everything I'd kept as her words wrapped around me.

If I had listened to my mind wanting to tell me it was a waste of time to be feeling my feelings, if I bought into the story that to feel them meant I was troubled, or if I pushed away the tender, vulnerable parts inside me, I wouldn't have had what ended up being a beautiful, healing experience.

On one card Mom wrote: *Please remember as you go through life to take these special things with you—the knowledge that you're capable, the faith to make your dreams real, the feeling that you're truly a person of worth . . . And the assurance that you are loved and always will be!*

On another she wrote: *When in doubt listen quietly to yourself, Lovingly Mom.*

And on another she wrote: *It sounds too simple, but everything really is for the best. All will work out for you. Take care of yourself. You're special.*

I could hear Mom's voice through her loving wisdom, and my heart cracked open and I felt held. The tears I felt weren't really of grief. They were of abounding appreciation. I was renewed and inspired. I felt strengthened and more confident. Mom wanted to come through that Saturday night to deliver me those messages. I needed them.

Sometimes, we think we need to know what our feelings mean before allowing ourselves to feel them to receive our healing. Our mind pressures us to have to make sense of it rather than allow what is ready to rise up to come out. We want to interpret our doubts, fears, and sadness, attempting to find the answers to our soulful questioning right away, even if it's unrealistic as humans to always understand why we're feeling what we're feeling.

Feelings offer us a deep connection with an inner awareness. An openness to explore them is what we're really after. When we let go of *having* to know, we create space for the energy to flow. When we feel stuck or unsure, it's okay to be uncertain. We can trust that if we keep asking questions rather than blocking them, what we're looking for to create change, when it's ripe and ready, will arise of its own accord. When in tune with our intuition, we are truly guided and protected.

But, when we seek, force, search, or race through our mind for the right next step with tension, we separate ourselves from the peaceful, easy, even joyful experience we can otherwise have. Meeting what makes us feel unsettled with curiosity, suddenly out of nowhere, steadiness appears. We question from our gut, not our head. And then, we *know*. We know, because *it just feels right*. Our body lights up. There's a wondrous, clear energy. From there, we can take action.

I've only publicly shared my paintings twice: once in an art show in Los Angeles, and once they were featured in an indie New York art magazine. I preferred to keep my creations close. They were my safe space, in which I could explore and express myself. Some people are moved by them. Many aren't. It's not their thing. Some find them to be too dark. Some think I need better drawing technique. Some say they look indigenous or tribal, but I'm not attempting that; it just comes from somewhere within me. But what others think doesn't matter, because what wants to come through when I paint has nothing to do with *me*. We're so used to focusing on what things "mean" about us rather than what they don't.

After decades of devoting myself to the creative process, I've learned what we create is who we are *not*. What we are is a channel, a passage for the current of creativity to come through. Just as with life, in every moment, every out breath, something departs, moving through us.

In the interview for the magazine, I was asked, "Your images are so raw, vibrant, and viscerally beautiful but, dark, too. How does beauty and darkness collide for you?"

I told Royal Young, the interviewer, who was also a painter and author, "I can't help but wonder, who are we to decide what's dark and what's light? And why live in that duality?"

Why do we judge anger, or pain, or grief, whatever, as dark? Where did we learn that we have to only be in the light? The beauty is in allowing ourselves to feel without interpretation. Then we allow room for what wants to be released. We may *feel* it, we may *think* it, but we're *not it*. It's just a movement through us.

Analyzing and searching for meaning puts us into our head and blocks our energy. Instead, our opportunity is to allow whatever wants to arise, even if it's scary, painful, or difficult at times. Without interference, we transcend into unbounded expansiveness. Our opportunity when we feel any emotion is to remind ourselves that it doesn't have to mean anything about us or the situation at hand—with this will come true freedom, love, and acceptance.

Have you ever been upset about something or feel like you want to cry, but you don't know why? And then you tell yourself you shouldn't feel the feeling because it doesn't make any sense? Or you search for the reasons from a psychological perspective? Or you feel upset because of what someone else has done that you don't understand? And then you set the feeling away for another time, or suppress, and then find yourself increasingly anxious, irritated, or aggravated? This is what happens when we search for meaning before feeling our feelings.

When I was thirty-three, while getting my counseling-psychology degree, I started learning from Michele how to teach intuitive painting. She taught me an invaluable lesson. Sometimes the painting students would call on the assistants when they were stuck or had a question. Michele's warning to me was *If you don't know how to answer a student's question, don't.*

At first, I thought this was because she worried I would answer wrong. But the more I trained, the more I realized that wasn't what it was about at all. When we try to pretend we know an answer to a question or prove what we're doing when we're uncertain, it's impossible to meet the moment without our ego. Sometimes, it isn't easy to admit we don't know, especially when we think we *should* know. Instead, our opportunity is to be more interested in joining the journey of discovery.

Confusion is another way our mind traps us. When we feel confused, we loop in an endless circle of meaning. There seems to be no way out. It's easier to see confusion in another as an observer. Their posture starts to sink inward and their foreheads crease and eyes narrow. They reach their hand up to cover their face, or scratch their head, or look up thinking the ceiling above may help them make sense of things.

If we ask, What am I feeling?, and our answer is confusion, it's important to remember that confusion is not a feeling. It's a defense mechanism as a way to avoid having to feel what's deeper. Our mind finds all kinds of tricky, complicated ways to keep us from something that it deems uncomfortable. But why does our mind get to decide for us? Why does it get to meddle with us in the first place?

After allowing whatever is blocking you to release, you can see with transparency. The truth is that your mind just doesn't understand that the more it protects you from having to feel, the greater your sense of confusion becomes. But when you touch the pure feelings of your heart within, they wash through, taking what was corroded with them. The same goes with creative energy. If you come to what you want to create in your life from your head, muscling your way through, you avoid the ability to sense what wants to emerge fluidly.

There's something so magnificently enchanted about stepping into the open unknown. This is where the new, surprising, unexpected elements come in. Things you wouldn't have thought about. Things you *couldn't know.* You open to a whole new experience with love. You relax and allow your life to flow.

You don't have to know what you are doing or to make sense of it. You can be curious about what you don't know, and allow the unexpected, delighting in the mystery, not trying to define anything.

EXERCISE
Stepping Out of the Mind

1. **The best way to unravel the mind's grip is to ask these questions:**

   1. What am I really feeling?
   2. With gentle permission, how might I explore it?
   3. What is it that I really need or want right now, and I didn't have to understand it?

2. **Don't force the answer. With curiosity and courage, allow the answers to float forward.** This will help open your gate to emotional freedom. In order to feel secure enough to feel your true feelings, don't insist on knowing reasons for why you're feeling them. Then, you won't have to struggle.

3. **Allow your feelings.** Feeling our feelings can be so terrifying. We think they could overwhelm us and take us over, and we worry we might lose control. So we hunker down, push away, and resist what we most want, which is ultimately our own happiness. Simply allow them. And by "allowing" them, I don't mean blowing them out of proportion and letting them overrun you. True feelings are easy and gentle when you are present with them. They rise quickly and then gently release. Feeling your feelings becomes the practice, and it's so simple you won't even realize it's happening.

4. **Explore these questions to experience a simple release:**

   - What if what I'm feeling isn't wrong or bad, or didn't have to make sense, or wasn't figure-out-able right now, and that was okay, and I could feel it anyway?

   - Can I be vulnerable without worrying about what it meant?

   - Could I let the feelings come and go without having a clue as to why I'm feeling them?

   - What if my mind didn't know but my intuition did?

5. **Imagine you are holding your own hand or giving your child self a loving hug.** In truth, underneath challenging feelings there lies a gentle, soft feeling that simply wants to be listened to. Perhaps it's a small, innocent, tender, and maybe even childlike, frightened part of you. Hold this part of yourself dear and keep it close. Could you take a few moments for yourself and be super tender with yourself? Where might your safe spot to do this be? In the shower or a bath? A gentle walk? Or could you just let the feelings arise right here, right now, while trusting they will pass quickly? Let them go. It doesn't have to be a big deal. Like a simple wave of energy: Up. Out. Vanished.

Inspiration

> *We either make ourselves miserable, or we make ourselves strong. The amount of work is the same.*
>
> —Carlos Castaneda

Another Saturday afternoon after the losses, when feeling lonely and down, I took my child self on a play date to see Picasso's sculptural exhibit. I was so turned on by it that I wanted to run home and paint for hours. I love how much permission Picasso gave himself. I was in awe of the breadth and freedom of his art, which he continued to make even when the Germans condemned him as a degenerate to remain in occupied Paris during World War II, forbidden to exhibit. When his art was considered debased and prohibited, it gave him all the more intention. He had to express himself, and he found any way to do it. One bronze sculpture I loved looked like a cow's skull with horns but was actually made from a scavenged bicycle seat and bike handles.

An online dictionary defines inspiration as:

> *Divine influence directly and immediately exerted on the mind or soul. A quickening, exalting influence. To produce or arise a feeling. To guide or control by divine influence.*

It's a sudden idea and a feeling you must do something—and then finding you have all the energy needed to do it. Doors open. It gives us a sense of "rightness," as if we can't *not* do it. We are guided by something greater coursing through us.

All art, the best museums, theaters, concert halls, designs, inventions, architecture, business brands, gardens, etc., were created to inspire and delight us. Without art, innovation, production, and nature, our lives would be dry, dull, lifeless, and without purpose. When we view art that moves us, we're uplifted. It's exciting and exhilarating, and we delight in the shared freedom of expression, feeling universally connected. But in order to stay in the flow, we need to connect back to our own divine influence. Inner inspiration comes when it's uniquely ours and individually inventive.

I rushed home from the museum and took the painting down that I'd been working on, curious to see what I would paint from Picasso's inspiration. I took a big, black brush and made a twisted face and a contorted nose. But quickly, I hit a major block and my energy dropped. I didn't want to paint anymore. If I wanted to be free like Picasso, I couldn't try to copy or act like I was him. I had to find the freedom of my own expression.

I went back to the painting that was up before I took it down. My brush got going. Returning to my own creation, I could meet my own insides where I was.

Comparison is a little death. It comes between inspiration and us. We think we need to hear the whole composition from beginning to end before composing it. Or know the entire arc of our story before writing it. Or have our whole business plan written before inventing our invention. Or know if the guy wants children and marriage before going on a second date with him.

How we keep our inspiration flowing is by giving ourselves permission to create whatever it is we're experiencing in the moment. The more we meet the moment, the more inspiration rains down upon us. But sometimes what's in the way of the current of inspiration coming through is a feeling we don't want to have. Our mind hates feelings, especially feelings deemed as bad. But we can't create what we want to create and not at some point meet up with uncomfortable emotions.

There are periods when there aren't lightning bolts of inspiration that strike. Instead, our life can feel like the same old, same old—stagnant and mundane. Our attention wanes. We lose interest in what we were once doing, or get bored. It's hard to snap out of it. But boredom is often just resistance, another clue we are ready to change.

When we're bored, we're afraid . . . of something. We're playing it safe. Tiptoeing around what we *really* need. Usually, it's something just underneath the surface that's being covered up. We've lost contact with our feelings and we stop because of self-doubt. Somewhere our subconscious starts delivering self-defeating messages. They may be faint. They may be loud. The trick is to become aware of the specific negative message that your mind is telling you.

Is your mind convincing you:

- I'm no good at this.

- I can't handle it.

- I'm not sure what I'm doing (and that's scary).

- It's harder than I thought it would be.

- Other people are better at this than I am.

- It doesn't matter in the bigger scheme of things.

- No one understands why this is important to me.

- I'm wasting my time, regardless.

What happens all too often is that we hear self-doubting thoughts and we believe them to be true without challenging them. We take them too seriously. We treat them as fact. We aren't aware of what we're covering up. We stop or we quit on ourselves. There's a difference between stopping and quitting. If we stop the flow of our life energy, we can choose to become aware of the judgment that's blocking us, and return to what we're doing. If we quit completely, we become paralyzed because we haven't tuned in to what our inspiration is providing. Whether you stop or quit, know this: Something inside you wants you to step up to a whole new level because creativity is meant to overcome self-doubt to build a greater sense of self.

While the Buddha was meditating, he became aware of a voice calling to him. He named this voice Mara, and the voice took on a personification. Whenever Mara appeared, the Buddha would look Mara in the eye and say, *I see you Mara.* As soon as Mara was seen, he vanished.

Even on the Buddha's deathbed, Mara came to tell him how great he was, how much he did for the world, how enlightened he had become, and how much help he had offered. The Buddha looked at Mara, said: *I see you*, and returned to the focus of his meditation. Even accolades are a distraction that can stop you from completing your creative journey.

Questions to ask:

- Can I return to what I started that for whatever reason I've stopped?

- Can I become aware of what my mind might be saying and then simply say back to it, "I see you," and continue on?

- Could I find new enthusiasm if I wasn't attached to the outcome?

The mind is always searching for definitive results. It wants assurance of where we're going, so it makes it difficult to continue into the unknown. But when we stay awake and aware, we remain open to surprises. We go somewhere we haven't been before. But we can't do that unless we move forward. The only way to be awakened is to bypass self-judgment. That's when the thunderbolts of inspiration come.

When we hear someone telling a joke, our mind races ahead, trying to guess the punch line. What makes the joke funny is the punch line we weren't expecting. What gets us most pumped up during a sports game is how we can't predetermine what will happen. We wait and anticipate a goal. The point is to open ourselves up to the possibility of creating something we can't even anticipate.

Sometimes when I'm painting, I get tired or indifferent. My strokes continue, I keep going for color and meeting brush to paper, but in reality I'm just plodding along. Nothing fun or exciting is happening. I want to stop painting. At this juncture, I know to ask myself this question: *What if something new could come in or out of the painting's images?*

When I ask this question, like when I'm doing a self-portrait, sometimes a fresh image will pop into my head like slithering electric yellow snakes through my rib cage, or lightning bolts hit my chest from every edge of the paper, or hands come in to grab me. *Yeah, let's go there!* I think: *Now I'm getting the energy moving.* Even though when I ask the question it can be scary, I'm awake again! When I ask, *What can possibly come in or out?*, a big energy rises up and is ready to leap out of its cave with a deep, booming roar. Now I have new open space to explore.

To really get out of boredom, apathy, and lethargy and find inspiration, it takes bravery, a willingness to wake the sleeping beast, look it right in its beady eyes, and face it squarely. Sometimes to stay the course you need to shake yourself to wake up.

Ask yourself:

- What if something new could come in or go out of my life?
- What if it could be anything? Big or small?
- What might be ready and calling me to wake up and shake things up?

There are many places where you can get stuck. It's important to accept these experiences as normal. These feelings say nothing about your project, your life, or you. Instead, these reactions can be an invitation to ask the big questions:

- What feels impossible to do right now?
- What seems so hard that I'm just not able to follow through?
- How might I take a big step toward it?

On the other side of "impossible" is great growth. When you meet what seems the hardest with loving kindness, you transcend into the field of unlimited possibility, and you'll soon discover a different you.

But why don't we challenge ourselves sometimes? Why is it easier to remain safe and secure in our inactivity or distractions? It's because you (and everyone else) feels fear, restless, and uneasy. The mind fills with limiting beliefs and it becomes so easy to fall prey to self-pity, which is the greatest form of self-neglect.

Whenever you hear the voice in your head asking, "Why . . .

. . . is this happening?"

. . . am I SO overwhelmed?"

. . . am I so tired?"

. . . don't I get it?"

. . . can't I do this?"

. . . is it SO hard?"

Pay attention to how you might stretch yourself. Check in to see if you can ask *how* instead of why. This will help you claim your power:

- How might I be creating this situation that is happening?
- How might I find more calm, peace, and ease?
- How could I open to receive more insight?
- How might I go about doing this with openness and curiosity?

EXERCISE
Getting Unstuck Quick

To counteract feelings of being stuck, I recommend you brainstorm what is most important to you right now in your life.

List the top five things that matter most to you.

1. _____

2. _____

3. _____

4. _____

5. _____

2. **Ask yourself if you're really making these top-five things a priority**. If not, then ask yourself these questions:

- How might I have what I really want in my life?

- How am I responding to this situation and others around me?

- How do I want to go about this differently?

- Is there something that I'm putting my time and attention on that is not in alignment with these priorities and that I should set aside or drop?

- How do I want to specifically create change and accomplish my priorities?

3. **Come up with a plan for your next course of action for each thing you chose**. What is one step you will take to embody these things that most matter to you? For example, if it's your family, how might you spend more time with them? If it's your health, how might you take better care of it? If you prioritize peace of mind, how would you create more well-being? How might this add more inspiration to your life?

Plan 1: _____

Plan 2: _____

Plan 3: _____

Plan 4: _____

Plan 5: _____

4. **Identify a new possibility.** Is there something that turns you on, excites you, or inspires you that could be added to this list? Perhaps something you don't make a priority but secretly desire to? What might that be? Could you make time for this as well and see what new, fresh inspiration could enter into your life currently?

....

Having assessed your priorities, you may have discovered that you've made some choices that are not in alignment with what is most important to you; for example, a daily decision, a type of relationship, a community commitment, or a career that strips the life out of you. You may ask yourself: *How did I get here?* And you stay because it feels like you can't renege on your decision. Or fear there isn't another option. Or you could disappoint someone. Or others depend on you. Or you depended on them. Or simply because you're a person of high integrity with morals and values, who follows through on their word and commitments. But your soul *knows* you are in the wrong place. You know what you need, but you may not know how to *have* it. It's in these times that you're asked to look deeper within. Reframing how you were once seeing things, you get closer to creating your dreams.

The greatest way to connect with inspiration and have a 360-degree view is to listen to the higher voice speaking to you, the voice of your creative intuition. When you pay attention and listen closely, you can hear the answer from insight rather than from the mind. It is then your heart will guide your course of action for change in your life.

You may think you should do something or have to do something based on your circumstances. In these situations, there could be two solutions. One, find a middle way that can work for you, creating more balance, boundaries, and time to take care of yourself, while remaining in the situation. Or two, give permission to shift gears, change course, and create a better option.

- Which direction would you choose if you listened to your creative intuition?
- Given both choices, which feels the most right to you?
- What if you took your losses, trusting there were better returns ahead of you?
- What if it's not the situation you're in but how you're relating to it?

- What if making you the priority might end up also being better for everyone else?

- What if you could create exactly what you want—however you want it?

Wherever you feel a contraction or a reaction—that's the place to question. A higher calling is asking something of you. Ultimately, the answer is already there. And you know it.

Creative Questions to Ignite New Inspiration

1. What book have you been reading, or movie you've seen, or art that's inspired, or podcast, or interview you've heard that you could get more of to help set you on the right path? What inspires you about doing this? Could you get more of these things in other ways?

2. If you were to tell your life story and share your life lessons, like growing up, leaving home, getting married, having kids, or starting over, what might writing this story bring you in regard to possible new life inspiration?

3. Is there a situation/habit/behavior you would like to stop/drop and, if so, could feel tons better? And what new obsession could you replace that with?

4. How might you get moving more? Exercise is a great place to clear your head and get inspiration. A cycle class with loud music to get your energy going? A good endorphin high to release the stuck spots in your mind and body?

5. What if you asked people what turns them on and gives them inspiration? Call five friends and ask them what excites them, and see if you're inspired to join them.

6. Is there a game you like to play? How about bringing more fun into your life? Learn the Tarot? A round of golf? Join a fencing competition?

7. Is there something you started that you enjoyed but put off that you could return to? Or what were you doing last year, or three, four, or ten years ago, that turned you on that you might investigate again?

8. Is there something you would like to teach? Have you overcome a certain challenge that you know you could help people with? Could you start a group?

9. Where do you get totally lost and absorbed? What can you do repeatedly without getting bored?

10. Is there something new you would like to research or study? What might this interest reveal to you?

    The list is endless once you get started. Try one. Try two. See where it leads you. Chase excitement. You'll feel the difference immediately. Plus, you never know what may come from it . . . possibly even a whole new you!

Presence

While I was a workshop junkie, living in Santa Fe in my late twenties, I had friends who were attending meditation retreats in various isolated places all over the world. They begged me to go with them.

No way! I'd say. *Hell to the no. I can't sit still in silence even if for a minute.*

I could focus on writing or painting in a quiet room, but the thought of being somewhere where it was enforced, in total silence, perhaps on top of a mountain for a weekend or more, made me fear I'd either go crazy or leap off the highest peak.

You could say I leaned toward drama in my twenties. I used to be an actress, after all. I wanted to have as much passion and adventure as I could. On a summer backpacking trip through Europe when I was twenty-four, I searched for *Happy Lynn* in between sips of rosé at European cafes, waiting for a hot Renaissance man with a symphonic accent to sweep me off my feet. When I spring vacationed in Hawaii, I tried to find *Laid-Back Lynn* dressed in brightly colored sarongs as I fantasized about getting stoned with blond, long-haired surfer dudes on the beach. (When in truth, I didn't even like to swim or smoke marijuana.) I worked very hard to become *Enlightened Lynn* as I explored every spiritual avenue I could, only to realize I was still human and would always have issues to work through. As I searched outside myself for my happiness, I avoided what needed to be met within.

When I was thirty-four and had graduated with my psychology degree, doing my internship as a counselor and just starting to date Shlomi, I was also required to be in therapy. I was referred to a counselor who happened to be a Buddhist teacher as well. After a few weeks of sessions, he gently pushed me to attend a weekend meditation workshop he was teaching at his counseling center in Los Angeles. He supported me to start meditating at home every morning for ten minutes to help prepare me for the weekend the following month. It was difficult, and my mind rarely settled, but I started to notice significant changes in how I was meeting myself. Meditation was offering me a safe container to allow whatever I was feeling to pass quickly.

A few months later, he encouraged me to come to one of his four-day silent retreats on Mt. Baldy in San Bernardino in the mountains of Southern California. After so many years of flat-out refusing, I thought I should prove to myself I could do it, even though I was terrified to go. It took me two days to settle in and relax my fear.

About twenty-five of us sat in a small cabin, on black cushions on top of wood benches with our backs against the walls (thank God; otherwise my back would have killed me) for four three-hour sits a day. We would meditate for forty-five minutes and then walk slowly for twenty, following our in-and-out breath, and repeat the structure again. Between sits, the monks would make us vegetarian meals that were surprisingly good, usually consisting of a cooked vegetable or salad, a starch-like pasta or rice, and a soup that we ate out of our own individual sets of three small bowls with a spoon. We weren't allowed to make phone calls, use the internet, or read any material other than Buddhist books. The bathrooms were outhouses, and the showers sprayed cold water. Yet, my tension from the city slowly dropped out as I accepted my commitment to being there. When I finally realized there was nothing else I could do but make the most of it, my fighting slowly dropped out.

I discovered peace in the yellow-pine forest, the pyramid peak of the summit with a steep south face, the highest point of Los Angeles, snow-capped across the road on a clear, bright day. I surrendered to beauty. With each three-hour sit, I generated more and more sustained focus and ultimately entered into that beautiful state of contentment that my friends had told me about.

One night, walking back to my small, one-person cabin that used to be Leonard Cohen's when he attended retreats there, I wondered how many songs he wrote in that very cabin, and what he dreamed of when he put his head on the very cot I slept on. I stared at the moonlit trees lining the road. There was a moment—a short moment, but a moment nevertheless—where I actually thought to myself, *I could live here forever. I need nothing else but to be here. Right now. Where I am.*

Soon afterward, I found myself craving frozen yogurt with dark chocolate chips, and blueberries, and immediately felt guilty.

Back inside my cabin, I wrote a list of all the things I missed in my journal. The white, Egyptian-cotton sheets on my king-sized bed; lavender-scented, candlelit baths; Thai ice tea; chatty conversations with my best friends; dancing to loud club music in my living room; soft, scrambled eggs . . . it was then I realized the ordinary *really* was extraordinary.

Since the contentment on the mountaintop wasn't my daily reality, I could come to appreciate the small things in my life that made me feel happy. I didn't need all that searching to make me feel as though I was living.

- What would be on *your* list? Which ordinary things are, in fact, extraordinary in your life?

- Which of those things might you enjoy more of to invoke the feeling of contentment?

- Is it possible that this might just be exactly what you need to experience right now to be your happiest?

Oprah asked Eckhart Tolle, author of *The Power of Now*, in an interview, "Are you enlightened? And if so, does that mean you're happy all of the time?"

His response was "Well, no. . . . I'd prefer to call it *peaceful aliveness.*"

After my silent retreat, I knew what he meant. Not that I'm enlightened, but because I could recall when I felt my best, and that wasn't necessarily in my most elated, euphoric moments. Mainly because those kinds of happy moments are fleeting and transitory; they pass by quickly and we return to our daily lives. I felt my absolute best when I was my steadiest, clearest, and most relaxed. By allowing more mindfulness and presence, our creativity is greatly affected. Becoming more focused, concentrated, and absorbed with inner balance and peaceful aliveness informs all our life endeavors.

My teacher/therapist taught me that while meditating, there were two "knobs," like on an inner stereo, for us to fine tune: excitation and torpor. *Excitation* is when we're aroused and revved up; our nervous system is overstimulated. Our opportunity is to turn the knob down a touch to find even ground. *Torpor* is when we're slacking, lethargic, sluggish, or lazy. Here, we have opportunity to dial the knob back up to focus, like splashing our face with cold water. The point is to find a calm, abiding equanimity, or, in laymen's terms, *balance*.

On the silent retreat, we practiced a Buddhist meditation called *Shamatha*. There are nine stages called the *jhanas*. For our purposes here, I'm only going to address the first four stages of the *jhanas* in an overly simplified version.

Once you become really focused and absorbed on the object of your meditation, like your breath, a visualization, a mantra, the center of your heart, a spot between your upper lip and under your nose, or whatever it may be, **you** encounter the 1st *jhana* when the palms of your hands or parts of your body start tingling from the sustained concentration.

In the 2nd *jhana*, you fill your heart with love for yourself and all beings, and that, combined with the electricity you feel in your body, can lead you to experience a kind of ecstasy.

In the 3rd *jhana*, you intend to drop the "body feeling" and stay in your heart center, finding a lovely space of contentment when you don't need anything or to be anywhere except for right there.

In the 4th *jhana*, you let go of contentment, and what happens next feels like falling into a deep snowbank, or dropping down to the bottom of a well. This stage is equanimity. It's that place of peaceful aliveness that Eckhart Tolle was talking about.

Guess which stage the Buddha was in when he reached enlightenment? Yep! The 4th. Not in the buzz, not in ecstasy, not in pure contentment, but in a beautiful place of serenity, like "nothingness." A calm-abiding sensation without the mind racing that feels very comforting. Nothingness doesn't mean you *feel* nothing. You *feel* vibrant. But your mind isn't involved. Thoughts are still there, but so faint you don't get caught in them. They're way, way in the background. And rather than thinking, true uninhibited, pure insight enters in. The heightened feelings or the stuck, heavy states have vanished and you're *level*.

It sort of seems like a big bummer, yes? If you're like me, I thought my whole goal in life was to be happy, only to then grow up and find out that our *true* happiness lies in simple peace. Inner balance means taking the day easy and allowing grace, while feeling luminous, present, and clear. Can you remember times when you felt this way? A summer day taking a walk around a lake? A cup of tea and a good book, being wrapped in a blanket by a fire on a winter evening? A day at work when everything just seemed to flow without drama, stress, or anxiety?

- What does peaceful aliveness mean for you?

- How might you cultivate it?

- How might this take the pressure off the need to strive for happiness?

Isn't it refreshing? In actuality, you don't have *to do* anything or *get* anything to live your best life.

The *Business Insider* published an article in January 2016 about a sixty-nine-year-old Tibetan Buddhist monk from France who's been called the world's happiest man. His name is Matthieu Ricard. What makes him the happiest man is that he participated in a twelve-year brain study on meditation led by a neuroscientist from the University of Wisconsin, Richard Davidson. "The scans showed that when meditating on compassion, Ricard's brain produces a level of gamma waves—those linked to consciousness, attention, learning, and memory—never reported before in the neuroscience literature," Davidson said. "The scans also showed excessive activity in his brain's left prefrontal cortex compared to its right counterpart, allowing him an abnormally large capacity for happiness and a reduced propensity toward negativity."

Matthieu Ricard says the reason why we're unhappy is altruism. His answer to finding happiness is to stop thinking "ME, ME, ME."

"It's not the moral ground," Ricard says. "It's simply that me, me, me, all day long, is very stuffy. And it's quite miserable, because you instrumentalize the whole world as a threat, or as a potential sort of interest [to yourself]."

I get this. When I thought negative thoughts or focused on my problems, I actually ended up inhabiting them. Sometimes this happened when I put my attention only on what I wanted to change in myself. I did this when I worried I wouldn't become the better person I wanted to be. But what I was denying with all that self-analysis was my happiness in presence.

The whole purpose of meditation is to train our mind, but if we train it to look only for what's wrong, what needs fixing, our issues—we feed our depression and anxiety. If we train ourselves to focus on joy, compassion, and kindness, then we have more joy, compassion, and kindness in our overall life.

Matthieu Ricard said, "With mental training, we can always bring [our level of happiness] to a different level. It's like running. If I train, I might run a marathon. I might not become an Olympic champion, but there is a huge difference between training and not training. So why should that not apply to the mind?"

So, what was his suggestion for increasing happiness? "Just spend fifteen continuous minutes a day thinking happy thoughts."

When I first started meditating, beginning with ten-minute intervals, I slowly, slowly increased to an hour daily. The practice was to raise my capability to concentrate by staying focused on the object of my meditation. Each morning, I began with a loving-kindness meditation, called *metta. Metta* is part of the "training" that Matthieu Ricard's referring to.

After I read an article about it, I was thrilled to add to my *metta* practice continuous thoughts about others and myself that made me happy. Who says happiness is a skill that can't be learned? And it needn't be something that is forced. It can be easy, a simple reminder to just put our attention on it.

I came to approach my grief and my creative process in the same way that I meet my meditation practice. The more I was present, the more I was able to meet what was in front of me, whatever stage of the process. The more I met the present, the more I surrendered to the flow, allowing it to breathe me rather than me breathe it. I wasn't aiming for peace or contentment, even though that's what came from it. It was the focus on the object at hand. Just like with life, whatever it is that we're creating with sustained attention makes us connect fully to the moment.

How to Do *Metta* Meditation

* For a recording of this to listen to while you're meditating and more, visit LynnNewman.com.

1. Sit in an upright chair with your feet flat on the ground and your hands palms down, resting on your thighs. Imagine that there is a cord of light running up from your pelvis out the top of your head. Pretend to gently tug at the cord at the top of your head as if it were a string that was straightening your spine. Drop your chin slightly. Gently soften your eyelids. Your inner ears. And your jaw.

2. Focus on your breath, and take one deep inhalation through your nose, filling your chest and expanding your lungs and rib cage. And exhale. Take another deep inhalation through your nose, filling your chest and expanding your lungs and rib cage. And exhale. And one more deep inhalation through your nose, filling your chest and expanding your lungs and rib cage. And exhale. Now allow your breath to gently flow without forcing.

3. Imagine in your mind's eye a being who is most easy to love. Fill your heart with the loving kindness for this being.

4. Now spread that loving kindness to your closet friends and family in your inner circle.

5. And then expand that loving kindness to your outer circle of community.

6. Spread the expansive feeling of loving kindness throughout the town or city you live in. Your country. Your continent. And then spread it around the whole world.

7. Now imagine in your mind's eye a teacher, mentor, or someone who has positively influenced your life, and then send them this loving kindness.

8. Imagine a stranger or a person who crossed your path recently, and send them loving kindness.

9. Imagine a difficult person, someone you may have conflict with or unresolved issues. Send them this force of loving kindness.

10. Now see an image of yourself and send yourself this loving kindness. This is a very important part of the process. Continue to send this loving kindness to yourself for many minutes.

11. If your mind drifts, just remember to lovingly and kindly bring your focus back. Soon, you'll be able to sit for longer periods of time without distraction.

14

Emptiness

> *Emptiness is the ground of everything. Thanks to emptiness, everything is possible.*

—Nagarjuna

When Mom was diagnosed with cancer, most of her remaining time was a spent waiting for news from recent tests, which could take weeks, for the next round of chemo, to hear if she was in remission, or for an appointment with her oncologist, who seemed to always be out of town on a fishing trip, or a bicycle race, or at his second home in Colorado. Yet, my mother never complained.

"Mom, how do you do this?" I asked her. "Isn't it hard to wait like this . . . in the unknown?"

She responded quickly, "That's what we all do, Lynn, all the time. That's what life is."

"But how can you be so patient?"

"That's all we *can* do. We have no other choice . . . one step at a time."

Mom was determined to build her strength daily by walking rounds on Seven West's floor at the Pink Palace, what she called the hospital painted pink on top of a hill overlooking our hometown of Tulsa. She carted her chemo drip, smiling, saying hello to all the nurses, and handing out bags of mini Snickers, Reese's Peanut Butter Cups, and Three Musketeers. She courageously made the most of her time.

For my Mom, it was more like "Don't sweat the *big* stuff." The small details were where she could gain some sort of control. She liked her coffee poured two inches into the cup and microwaved in the nurse's kitchen for exactly thirty seconds. Her day planner, ChapStick, and crossword puzzles were stacked neatly to the left on the hospital bedside table. The phone sat on the bed, next to her hip for easy access. She came to know all the nurses by name, whom she liked and whom she didn't, who was helpful and who wasn't, sometimes expecting care as though she were actually in a high-end spa, but most of the time she was resigned to the circumstances.

"I'm inspired by you, Mom," I wrote to her, among other things, in an email. "You're so brave." I was astonished by her ability and courage to meet emptiness, especially in the face of death.

Emptiness is a buzzword in Buddhism. Westerners have misunderstood this word to mean "a void." And that's what we're really afraid of, being sucked up into some kind of black hole. But what "emptiness" really means in the Buddhist sense is *spaciousness*, *boundlessness*, and *connectedness*. As a culture we're so used to grasping in order to achieve. We see emptiness as crushing rather than freeing. But emptiness is full of life.

Our misunderstanding of emptiness is what stops us from meeting the present. It's why we hold on to the past or project into the future. Why we do anything, actually, to avoid the here and now—because then, we would have to face the terrifying unknown. We try to soothe that fear by filling the space with whatever we can: Sugar. Our horoscope. Relationships. Approval. Work. Chatter. Screens and social media. The news. We do everything we can to focus on what's going on "out there," not to miss out on anything, trying to get something outside us to fulfill us, some sort of understanding or validation, rather then seeing our opportunities to meet ourselves within and experience what lives *there*. Frankly, getting to know our own insides is just too uncomfortable. We're afraid of what we might find and be forced to feel it.

When we first sit down in the morning at our desk with a pile of papers and a long to-do list, we can feel trepidation or panic. Meeting a white piece of paper or staring at a blinking cursor takes tremendous fearlessness, which is one reason so many historically great writers, when faced with a blank page, were prone to drink. They attempted to soothe their fear and fill the unknown that creativity asked them to consciously meet. But *they didn't have to suffer in the name of art*. Our opportunity is to see our thoughts as if they were like clouds moving across a great sky. When we look up at the infinite sky and feel its spaciousness, what do we really experience inside?

We might feel:

- Openness

- Expansion

- Relaxation

- Lightness or floating sensations

- Fluidity and flow

- Calmness

- Peace

When we meet emptiness, we connect to something much greater. A current of energy awakens in us. Loneliness and anxiety subside. Our hearts expand. We feel in love with what we're doing, with others, with life. This is what happens when we step through fear. This is what's on the other side. *If only we could know this and trust it.*

We'd show up every day ready to meet our list, our chores, our work, our relationships, the empty canvas, our many emails, or the Word document. We'd feel safe in stillness and silence. We'd delight in the uncharted. We'd feel calm in the uncertainty of our future or even peace in the face of death. But this seems a grand thing to ask of us. After all, we only know what we've experienced. Most of us, if not all of us, are more comfortable with what's familiar. And what we know best is fear. Love scares the bejesus out of us, so fear is the most pervasive.

Elizabeth Kübler Ross, author of *On Grief and Grieving*, writes: "There are only two emotions: love and fear. All positive emotions come from love, all negative emotions from fear. From love flows happiness, contentment, peace, and joy. From fear comes anger, hate, anxiety, and guilt. It's true that there are only two primary emotions, love and fear. But it's more accurate to say that there is only love or fear, for we cannot feel these two emotions together, at exactly the same time. They're opposites. If we're in fear, we are not in a place of love. When we're in a place of love, we cannot be in a place of fear."

What if I told you, promised you, that if you met that thing you fear and continued through it, you would not only be okay, you'd flourish? That you'd feel better than you've ever felt or could know was even possible?

I don't have to promise you because you've already had times in your life when you've experienced this. When you've checked several things off your list, how great did you feel? Or when you left a job you hated, or your fingers gained speed on your keyboard, or you danced with such freedom you felt like you could fly? It's an obstacle you have to get over. That moment you want to turn away from but need to step forward into instead. And then, the possibilities are endless.

You know people too, people who have faced their terrors and overcome with courage, who have inspired us as a world to continue and persevere under all circumstances: Nelson Mandela, who spent eighteen years in a small cell and was forced to do hard labor, to then end apartheid. Helen Keller, who was the first blind person to get a graduate degree to then campaign on social welfare, women's suffrage, and disability rights. Beethoven, who, even when he started to lose his hearing, composed some of the most beautiful symphonies the world has ever heard. J. K. Rowling, who was on benefits as a single mother and rejected by several publishers, only to become the world's bestselling children's author. Or Rosa Parks, who refused to give up her bus seat.

Over the course of my seven-year marriage, from ages thirty-five to forty-two, I went on retreat three times a year. Two of the retreats were for four days, and one was ten days every June. Even though before every retreat I was always nervous, I knew I would benefit. It's what helped me cope. In fact, it was on the retreats where I got clear about what I really wanted in my life and reconnected with the inner strength I needed to make significant inner and outer changes.

My teacher spoke about the importance of fully meeting beginnings, middles, and endings. The first night we came to a retreat, all of us bustling with nervousness and anticipation, trying to let go of the tension from the rush-hour traffic, he reminded us to be present with *arriving*. Halfway through the retreat, when it's common to start missing life down the mountain, like hump day during the workweek, he reminded us to be present with *middles*. On the last day of retreat, we would still have our morning three-hour meditation sit. Afterward, we would meet together as a group and break our silence for the first time to share our experiences. Typically, I started leaving the mountain mentally as I began packing the previous night. I couldn't wait to sleep in my own bed, catch up with friends and family, and get back to the gym after all that sitting. In my last hours of meditation, I had to remind myself to be more present with *endings*.

Of course, while meditating quietly, my mind still found ways to mess with me: the irritations of the itch at the tip of my nose that had to be scratched, the fly that had to be shooed, the cramp in my knee that had to be adjusted, the crick in my back. I learned that if I didn't move, allowing whatever minor or major pesky interference to pass, I could meet emptiness and reach that blissful space of total absorption relatively fast, where discomfort no longer existed. It seemed impossible when I first started. But the payoff was grand, and generating sustained focus was always worth it.

The hardest times were when I returned to everyday life without the serenity and protective atmosphere of the retreat and the mountain. Distraction and my emotional reactions could get the best of me. After realizing the deep, loving concentration I was truly capable of, real-life moments of interference could be very painful.

As soon as we become aware of the loss of our attention, our opportunity is to *simply, kindly, and gently return our focus*. Without shaming, wronging, or scolding ourselves. Without guilt or regret. Without feeling sorry for ourselves or allowing our inner judge telling us it's too hard or "I can't." When we catch ourselves drifting away because of our fear of emptiness, all we need to say is *Oops! There I went! No problem. I'm just going to go back.*

If you lose your target, it's not a big deal. It's not an issue that needs analysis. It says nothing about who you are and your capabilities. It doesn't mean you aren't good enough; it doesn't mean that you're bad or not a success. When you find yourself falling off focus, just gently, kindly, lovingly course correct. The more times you keep compassionately coming back, the more you create relaxed, sustainable, determined attention. The more attention you accumulate, the easier it is to meditate. Obviously, this isn't only about meditation practice. You can apply this to everyday life as you learn to work with your mind's interferences.

My older brother, Russ, has tinnitus, a condition that causes ringing and buzzing in the ears. He was helping build a house for Habitat for Humanity, and while using a power drill his ear went POP. Ever since that day he has a ringing in his head that just won't stop. Nor will it ever. I cannot imagine what this must be like to live with. I see his face scrunch with discomfort when he's eating in a restaurant that's too loud, and how he struggles to stay a part of the dinner conversation.

He's spent years trying to find a remedy, from white noise, to sound boxes, to building a kit car to keep his mind off things, to researching and seeing experts to try and get some sort of relief. I wish I could just crawl into his ear and whisper sweet things, telling him it'll be all right and that he's safe and loved.

One day, he excitedly called me to tell me he met with someone, a specialist in tinnitus who had some advice. She told him to give this noise in his eardrum a name and to talk to the noise. To tell the noise he hears it but to take a back seat, because he's the driver now. I couldn't help but think how that same advice applies to the chattering, critical voice in our head and the importance of taking our power back.

To say, *Dude, I hear ya' but we're gonna be doing something else now. I'm grateful you have so much to say to me because you're challenging me to grow, but right now I'm choosing peace instead.*

It's like when the distracted mind pulls my attention everywhere but the focus of the meditation. The goal is to stay focused on the object (my breath, a mantra, a visualization, my heart center, etc.) and not waiver to create an enduring sense of calm. But of course, my mind still drifts. So when it does, I can say firmly, *Hey, let's bring ourselves back*. And then make it happen.

It reminds me of housebreaking a puppy. Training experts have proven that scolding and yelling *No! Bad boy!* can cause negative consequences. It's just like how the negative reinforcement of punishment can harm a kid. If you have or have had a puppy, you know it takes months to train them and loads of patience. There's this one way to train where you take their paw and hit it on a bell hanging from the door before taking them outside to do their business. When they learn it, they will signal you. Every time you catch yourself caught in the noises in your head and lovingly refocus, it's like a puppy's paw hitting a bell. That returning then becomes the practice. And the more you return, the more the humming in your ear fades into the background.

You don't have to meditate to learn how to do this, although it does help. You can do it all the time whenever and wherever you are, *if* you remember. The more attention you cultivate, the less those mind buggers get to rule you. It may be a painful ringing you might never be able to be free from, but with time, you can learn to lessen its blow by turning down the knob "just so."

A Meditation
to Create Calm Concentration

* For a recording of this to listen to while you're meditating and more, visit LynnNewman.com.

1. Sit in an upright chair with your feet flat on the ground and your hands palms down, resting on your thighs. Imagine that there is a cord of light running up from your pelvis out the top of your head. Pretend to gently tug at the cord at the top of your head, as if it were a string that was straightening your spine. Drop your chin slightly. Gently soften your eyelids. Your inner ears. And your jaw.

2. Focus on your breath and take one deep inhalation through your nose, filling your chest and expanding your lungs and rib cage. And exhale. Take another deep inhalation through your nose, filling your chest and expanding your lungs and rib cage. And exhale. And one more deep inhalation through your nose, filling your chest and expanding your lungs and rib cage. And exhale. Now allow your breath to gently follow without forcing it.

3. Focus your attention on the center of your chest as you feel your lungs expand out toward your rib cage. As you observe your lungs expand outward on your inhale, count one. As you observe your lungs contract, count one. Then, as they expand again, count two. And contract two. Expand three. Contract three. And so on. If you lose track, lovingly begin again.

4. Now focus your attention on the air that is moving in and out of your nose. As you feel the air moving out of your nose, count one. As you feel the air inhale into your nose, count one. As it moves out, count two. As it moves in, count two. As it moves out, count three. As it moves in, count three.

5. Now focus on a small spot at the top of your lip. Keeping your attention on this spot at the top of your lip, observe your breath. As you inhale, count one. As you exhale, count one. As you inhale, count two. As you exhale, count two. As you inhale, count three. As you exhale, count three.

6. Allow your attention to rest on this small spot at the top of your lip for as long as you can, keeping your focus. If you lose focus, gently and kindly return back to the spot at the top of your lip.

Impermanence

> *Everything is in process. Everything—every tree, every blade of grass, all the animals, insects, human beings, buildings, the animate and the inanimate— is always changing, moment to moment.*

—Pema Chodron

The two days before my father died, when I was thirty-eight, I meditated on the floor next to his bed at home. Somehow, when Dad was conscious he found the strength to lift his weak body up and grab my cheeks like he always did when I came down the stairs for Shabbat dinner as a child. He was unable to speak, but he mouthed the words with full-cupped lips, "I. Love. You." I received these words, a balm over my heart.

Mom was in their shower when Dad died. My brother Marty and I were sitting by Dad's side. Shlomi had gone to run an errand. I wondered what was taking him so long.

It was obvious Dad was going soon. I think Mom couldn't bear it.

"I read that when someone dies, you can hear the rattle from their lungs," I told Marty, both of us sitting next to Dad on the carpeted floor next to the bed, on our knees. It seemed a strange thing to say, but I was reading a Buddhist book at the time called *The Tibetan Book of Living and Dying* by Songyal Rinpoche. The book suggested that the whole purpose of meditation, ultimately, is to prepare for death, and I wanted to prove I was ready to witness my father's.

The amount of time Dad and I spent together his final month was so meaningful, but I also knew he was ready to be relieved from the body he was suffering in. I knew that just like Dad lived his whole life, he would want me to see the positive in this hard experience too.

"I don't know what you're talking about," Marty said.

"The rattle. It happens. Watch. There it is! You hear it?" In times of crises or trauma, I tended to want to be strong, trying to connect with my spiritual side.

I saw my father's eyes click toward the sunshine coming in through the window of my parents' bedroom. He was gone.

"Mom, it's time!" I raised my voice so she could hear but not too loudly to disturb Dad's passing.

"What?" she yelled from the bathroom.

"It's time!"

"Oh shit," Mom exclaimed through the bathroom door. "Marty!" she yelled for my brother.

Mom's plan was ready. She went to the kitchen, putting everything that needed to be medically recycled, hospice leftovers, needles, and pills into a plastic bin, quickly trying to rid herself of the pain, and covering it. We all handle grief in different ways. I wondered how my own avoidance to feel my feelings, perhaps even spiritually, was alike to the way Mom was dealing.

Per Mom's organization, Marty got on the phone to call family and community members. The funeral would happen that morning within two hours. Mom wanted it to be over as soon as possible. Shlomi and my brother Russ went to the mortuary, picked out the coffin, organized the funeral, and contacted the rabbi.

As everyone went off to do his or her jobs, I wasn't given one. I sat by Dad, not wanting anything else to do other than to be with him. My Buddhist teacher had told me that a body's spirit still lingers in the room for many hours. I wanted my father's spirit to see me there. He lay peacefully looking out the window as I waited for the ambulance and felt the energy in the room waver.

When the paramedics came and an EMT passed her hand over my father's face, closing his eyes, I realized we were now at the end. Dad had left. Two teenagers from the mortuary, with dyed black hair and wearing black eyeliner, came to lift Dad onto a trolley and bag him up. I followed Dad to the door and out into the driveway in my pajamas and bare feet.

"Mom! Marty! Dad's leaving," I cried. Dad was rolled out into the back of an old, black Cadillac hearse, and I waved goodbye like a child who had let go of a balloon, watching it float up into the sky.

When I went up to the rabbi at the Rose Cemetery in Tulsa just three hours later, I told him, "We are all of the nature to die and decay. Life is about impermanence." This Buddhist teaching was new to me then, helping me to cope.

"Yes, yes," the rabbi said as he nodded his head. I felt his sympathy.

It helped me to say this because death happens to all of us, in all forms, and I wanted some sort of a resolution. If I didn't, I would live my life in fear of our greatest opponent, death, and wouldn't be able to truly *live*, even though I was only thirty-eight at the time.

Yet, after the funeral was over, my spiritual resources failed, and my Dad's death devastated me. I grieved terribly, not able to rise out of bed or the dark. Dad had been my anchor, my rock, my stability. Without my father, I would have to learn how to face life on my own and grow up somehow, finally. Dad was no longer there to protect and take care of me. But I attempted to face Dad's death with courage, inspired by what he said to me a few days before dying, "I have no regrets."

Four years later, when I was forty-two, after Dad's passing, my four miscarriages, and knowing that my marriage was crumbling, I drove fast on Interstate 44 to the Pink Palace. The rain was coming down so hard I couldn't see through the front windshield. The wipers at their highest level were of no help. The car's defrost was on high too, but still I was blinded. I thought I should pull over, but I had to get to Mom.

I pulled into the parking lot, grabbed my purse, and ran through puddles as large as lakes. I burst through the sliding glass doors, up the escalator, into the foyer, and to the elevator. I sprinted down the oncology hall on Seven West and slowed down in front of the nurses' desk. Taking in slow, deep breaths, I tried to quiet myself. In front of Mom's door, I stopped and felt my feet on the floor.

The door was cracked. A faint light shone from the corner. I saw a nurse standing at the side of her bed. I heard my mother's faint voice.

"Come in," the nurse waved.

I wasn't ready. The nurse didn't know I needed to sneak in. I knew if Mom saw me appear suddenly, it would upset her. My presence was a sign that her time was near.

"Come in. It's okay," the nurse said.

I pushed the door with two fingers and slid in sideways.

"I was just leaving," the nurse encouraged me.

We passed by each other as I walked to the blue-green plastic-covered seat and sat my bag quietly down.

"Hi Mom," I said in my most quiet, sweet voice.

"Oy," Mom said, closing her eyes tightly. She knew if my brothers had called me to come home, my arrival meant she was coming to the end. She was dozing but conscious. I checked the drip; although she was on heavy meds, they hadn't started the morphine yet.

I rested my hands on my thighs like I sat in meditation every morning. I closed my eyes. Slowed my breath. Settled my fast-paced heart. My leather jacket was soaked from the rain and was too stiff to sit comfortably. I would need to take it off but knew it would disturb Mom. I looked at the clock on the wall. I closed my eyes again.

I filled my heart with light. The same way I did for Dad when he was dying. I let it expand through me and out to Mom, lying there. I wished her love. I wished her ease. I gave her my prayers. My everything.

When I opened my eyes and noticed the wall clock, it had been a half hour. I looked to see if my mother was sleeping so I could take my jacket off and perhaps curl up to stay the night. I slowly unzipped, but I woke her up. She lifted her head slightly and stared at me. Even though the room was dim, I could see her hazel eyes, glowing.

"Please leave," my mother said, shaking her head side to side. "Please, please leave!" I knew what was happening. Mom wasn't ready. She seemed hopeless, terrified.

"Okay, Mom. I'll go." I stood at the end of her bed.

Marty, Russ, and I took eight-hour shifts for her remaining seventy-two hours. On my first shift, Mom spoke to me in a drugged haze only once.

"Where's Shlomi?" she asked.

"He's in LA. He can come anytime. Would you like me to call him?" He wasn't there because we both already knew our plight.

She lifted her hand a tad and waved her fingers. "No. No. He has things to do."

I slept on the couch next to her and jumped up whenever she moved to see what she needed or what I could do.

I knew it was time when I saw her breathing change.

"Watch her carefully," I told Marty at the end of my shift.

Two hours later, Marty called. "Come now, but don't rush. You won't get here in time." When I arrived, Marty was holding her hand and gently crying. She had passed. Mom lay white, her mouth partially opened. Russ arrived a few minutes later with his wife.

For my birthday the following year, Mom had left me a card. Rather than a paper envelope, she crafted one made of fabric and closed it with a safety pin. Stuck to the outside of the handmade envelope was a Post-it with her instructions: *Don't open before Sept 2nd.*

Inside the card it read, *This wish is for your birthday. The love for you is always. May it be a great year Sept. 2nd to Sept. 2nd, Lovingly, Mom.*

I knew she intended for me to have a birthday card to open from her for the rest of my life.

Two months after Mom died, Shlomi had moved out and we'd signed our divorce papers. I slept with Lita every night, holding her close to my chest. So grateful I wasn't alone in the house and still had my baby.

But only a short month later, Shlomi and I sat on a tattered brown couch with burgundy pillows, and a wood-framed painting of two sleeping puppies was on the wall in front of us. Through the window, a sign hanging from the ceiling in the hall blared, *Quiet Please. Euthanasia Happening.*

Moments passed as we stared at the painting. I tried to decide if it was morbid or comforting, and then refocused my attention.

"Let's call in the light because that's who Lita really is. She's going back home. She's being freed from this body that no longer serves her. We'll help release her," I said.

"Okay," Shlomi said and started to cry. "But why is this happening? On top of our divorce?"

"It doesn't matter. This isn't about us right now. This is about Lita." I wanted to be a strong parent.

"Right," he said.

The veterinarian came and placed Lita on my lap.

"Bye, Lita," Shlomi cried.

"Ready?" The veterinarian said, "This one will put her to sleep."

Lita's eyes were already closed. I tried to feel her heart still beating through the thick towel between us.

"Now I'm going to give the second one." I watched to see if I could tell the difference.

"Okay. She's gone," the veterinarian said.

Lita's head rested to the side, falling into deep blackness.

"You can take her," I told him.

The veterinarian slid his hands under the towel, lifted her, and went toward the door.

I rose and walked out of the animal hospital. Shlomi kept up behind me, unlocking the car doors with an empty electronic beep. I sat inside.

"Don't drive. I'm not ready yet," I told Shlomi.

Staring through the parking lot, I saw trees across the road. I looked at the green and sat completely still. Energy in the air flickered. I couldn't move. I could see the particles shimmering in the sky between the trees. I felt my spirit lift behind, in front of, underneath, and above me. A small yellow leaf flitted down, tracing the particles in the air. I had practice now with impermanence.

Going out of being, I thought to myself, remembering my meditation practice. *That leaf . . . Lita's breath . . . everything and all goes out of being. The sound of the car that just passed . . . going out of being, Shlomi's slight move of his leg . . . out of being. Everything and all will eventually pass. That moment and now that*

. . . each second . . . out . . . out . . . out . . . I too will die. One day, at one time, I too shall pass.

I felt Lita there with me, her spirit surrounding with the most luminescent light filling the car. Light was all I could see. Everything goes out into the light. The light was always within me.

"I'm ready now," I said to Shlomi.

He carefully started the engine. Driving home, I watched everything pass us by. The light changing green, the seconds on the dashboard clock ticking, the breeze from the cracked window, another leaf falling, and another. I sat in silence the whole way home and breathed. Peace took over me.

Walking in the door without Lita there to greet to me, I went directly into the backyard and looked at the trees. Shlomi sat with me for a little while at the porch table, but I knew that too would soon come to an end, and it would be the last time I saw him.

I remembered my father and how his eyes clicked to the right toward the sunshine after taking his final breath. I remembered my mother and how she loved nature. How all she wanted to do her last year was to look out her window and see her maple trees. I remembered the mountain on meditation retreats and how the pines seemed to breathe, guiding me toward serenity.

Everything that comes into being goes out of being. We all decay. All things shall pass, and I knew in that moment that that too would pass, and the next, and the next, for the upcoming years, for the rest of my life. This was the only certain thing.

I thought to myself, *That is love*: to love with an open hand, an open heart, an open mind, offering it to the unknown. I realized then that love is in the moment when one is present, fully with nothing to hold on to except space and emptiness. Love exists in No-Thing-Ness. No husband. No dog. No Daddy. No Mommy. No baby. No body. No breath. No self. Love is not the air we breathe. Nor the breath we do not breathe. Love is abundant in everything and no thing. When left with nothing, there is nothing but pure Love.

I placed my hands over my eyes and cried into them. Nothing was left, except me, wholly to myself. Me and me. Nothing else.

I stood from the backyard table and went to my meditation cushion. I set the timer for forty-five minutes and crossed my legs, resting my palms face down on my thighs, straightening my spine and closing my eyes. I filled my body with light; my heart swelled with the love I felt for all. The love I felt for my parents. My love for Shlomi. The babies I'd lost. Renee, the woman who gave birth to me. And Lita was there too. They all were, beating inside my chest, expanding outward in infinite directions. They were not of me but moved through me, each and every one of them. They rested in the light, in the center of my beating chest. Not of me, by me, or for me, but through me, I learned to love.

A Meditation to
Rest in the Center of Your Heart

* For a recording of this to listen to while you're meditating and more, visit LynnNewman.com.

1. Sit in an upright chair with your feet flat on the ground and your hands palms down, resting on your thighs. Imagine that there is a cord running up from your pelvis out the top of your head. Pretend to gently tug at the cord at the top of your head, as if it were a string that was straightening your spine. Drop your chin slightly. Gently soften your eyelids. Your inner ears. And your jaw.

2. Focus on your breath and take one deep inhalation through your nose, filling your chest and expanding your lungs and rib cage. And exhale. Take another deep inhalation through your nose, filling your chest and expanding your lungs and rib cage. And exhale. And one more deep inhalation through your nose, filling your chest and expanding your lungs and rib cage. And exhale. Now allow your breath to gently breathe itself without forcing it.

3. Imagine above your head a bright sun full of radiating light.

4. From that sun, imagine a column of light pouring down into the top of your head and running straight down through your spine. Spread the light through your whole body. Fill your heart.

5. Now imagine a sphere of light surrounding your body above, underneath, and all around you. Make this sphere the size of the room you are sitting in. Expand it even further. As far as you can expand.

6. Sense the column of light through your body, in your heart and the sphere around you. Combine the light, allowing the light in your body to spread throughout the sphere and the sphere's light to spread into you.

7. See rays of radiating light throughout the sphere, and small particles of light flash throughout the sphere.

8. Rest in the light for as long as possible.

Identity

> You need not know who you are . . . for what you are cannot be described,
> except as total negation. All you can say is, "I am not this. I am not that."
> You cannot meaningfully say, "This is what I am."

—Sri Nisargadatta Maharaj

After all the losses, at age forty-two, I kept asking myself, *Who am I now?* I wasn't going to be a mother. I was no longer a wife. I was orphaned. I had no idea about my future, where I was going, what my life would become, if I would ever be in relationship again, or if I would be alone the rest of my life. But the answer couldn't come by asking that question. In fact, it eventually came from *not* answering it. As soon as I asked the question *Who am I now?*, the *Who am I now?* was already gone, slipping between my fingers, in the past already.

The question to ask is *Who am I not?*

This may seem super esoteric. But it's so simple and so close our mind simply doesn't know what to do with it. This question forces us to let go of everything we know so that we can discover the truth of ourselves. Sometimes we put so much attention on trying to figure it out that we can't see it.

In the midst of feeling like I was losing myself, no longer knowing who I was anymore, I discovered I was coming closer to my core. I was being stripped of the layering accumulated throughout my lifetime—beliefs, lies, and distortions that I learned to carry, covering who I truly was. I came to understand that every time I questioned, "*Who am I?*," it was a sign I was closer to knowing the answer of "who I was" deeper within than ever before. Even though my life was completely disrupted and I was off swimming, sometimes flailing, sometimes feeling like I was drowning, I learned how to let go of having to know who I was more and more. Releasing the need to have to know set me free—always changing, always dying, and always being reborn.

A few months after Mom and Lita died and Shlomi moved out, I put the house that we lived in together in Los Angeles on the market, desperately wishing to start anew. My neighbor Ethan approached me on the street. He had also lost his mother, knew Shlomi, and had some advice for me. His passion was playing Spanish guitar, and Spain was a second home to him. He told me that after his mother died, he sold one of his beloved guitars but deeply missed it. He warned me not to do anything major right after a big loss and strongly advised me not to sell the house.

Ethan's insight was spot on. I was traumatized, and moving right away would have been too much on my nervous system. It became very apparent that what I needed most was to take it easy and self-nurture. To go within, restore, and regenerate.

In times of change it's good to ask yourself:

- What is the gentlest, loving, and kindest way I could be with myself?
- What does my body or spirit need more of?
- What if I didn't have to fill the empty space with something else?
- What if I could let myself rest, be quiet, and take some down time for myself?

As the ebb of life flows, there are sometimes slow-moving streams and still pools. Like with nature, we can't force the river. I did everything I could during that time to do grounding, simple things like upping my meditation, taking slow, easy walks, and soaking in long baths to soothe me. I allowed myself to appreciate and respect the natural unfolding of change in my life. With trust, I came to the understanding that I needed to gestate and prepare inwardly for the new to birth itself. An apple that's not ripe can't fall from the tree. The positive change we want doesn't always happen in the timing we want. Hanging out in space can be frightening. But what if we trust that what's for our highest good will come at the moment we are truly ready?

A Checklist
to Ground while in Transition

1. **Find nature.** Be in it as much as you can. Use the energy and presence of trees to ground you. Feel your feet as you walk. Search for flowers and leaves and critters to raise your frequency.

2. **Seek stillness and silence.** Turn off the news, TV, social media, YouTube, etc. Find a room that is the quietest to spend some time in every day.

3. **Experience the elements.** Use fire (incense, candles, sage, fire pits, etc.), water (drink, bathe, steam, shower, wash, and moisturize face/neck/body), earth (sit, walk, rest, do yoga, ground in meditation), and air (deep breathing, focus on the breath in meditation, take in fresh air outside, etc.).

4. **Eat sustaining foods that keep you light and give you energy.** Eating heavy processed foods, sugar, and flour can really mess with your sense of vitality. Take care of your body during this time. Warm vegetables, legumes, and grains comfort as well as support digestion.

5. **Be physical.** Stretch. Work out. Get your endorphins releasing—it's a great natural high.

6. **Spend time with people you love.** Maybe even enjoy the silence together without needing to gab or do anything.

7. **Meditate and, at the end of each meditation, open your eyes, look around, and state out loud everything you are grateful for.**

8. **Question.** As emotional or physical stress arises, ask yourself in each moment:

    *   How might I experience this with peace?
    *   How might I be loving and tender with my child self?
    *   How might I choose a sweet, caring way of holding it?

If you grasp on to something like needing to know what's next, you can make the process of being in transition much harder. When you're afraid of the unknown, you can tend to want your answers now more than ever. The goal is not to flee from emptiness, but to loosen your grip and relax into the gap. The idea is to honor the passage of transition without reaching and allowing the beauty of the next phase of your life to arise according to its own divine timing.

Two years later, I was forty-four and ready to move, much stronger inside myself. I found a lovely small bungalow to rent in the Santa Monica canyon, with a partial ocean view, so I put the old house back on the market. While in escrow, the rental house in the canyon fell through. The owner had decided *she* didn't want to move. I didn't know what to do.

I ran into Ethan again on our street corner. He saw the escrow sign in my front yard and asked me where I was moving. I told him about my dream rental that was no longer available.

"I have no clue," I told him. "I guess I'll have to ask my movers to put everything I own in storage."

"Lynn, when is the next time you're going to have everything in storage and not have a mortgage to pay? You should go somewhere else for awhile, somewhere you've always wanted to . . . like the coast of Spain!" His eyes lit up talking about the dream of his own desired adventure.

I went inside my house and drew a bath. Placing my head back to soak, the idea floated forward: *New York City.*

When I graduated from high school, I was sure I'd end up at the Tisch School of Arts at NYU to major in theater instead of at the California Institute of the Arts in Southern California. After restoring myself for the two years postdivorce and loss, I was ready for new energy, and there isn't a city in the world that has the energy of New York.

I put everything in storage, packed two bags, and found myself in the Big Apple six weeks later, just like Annie did as she entered the stage, holding a suitcase, and "looked up at the top of the Chrysler Building," singing, "NYC! Too busy. Too crazy. Too hot. Too cold. Too late! I'm sold. Again. On NYC."

I couldn't believe I had moved across the country. I learned a valuable lesson in regard to my practical plan making. No matter how much I tried to plan, life didn't always work out the way I thought it would. It's common sense that we can't stay attached to our plans, really, because we all know that even when we try, life can change course, even when we prepare, think things out, and take our best action. I challenged myself to meet the current as it changed in front of me. Life has a funny way of showing the right path, eventually.

After being on the West Coast for most of my adult life (except for a few years in Santa Fe in my late twenties), this was a huge surprise to me—a life experience I didn't know was available. It was like some unknown force was leading me; my willingness and intuition guided me. I was being led somewhere better than even I believed.

So many times we think we have to *make* something happen. It's not that we should stop trying to be productive or lose sight of our goals, desires, or needs, but sometimes "doing" overrides "allowing." I often wondered what it would be like if I attempted to *not* do—to see what would happen next. Where I might end up without all that effort. I see clearly now that something larger than me had a plan of its own: A different city on a different coast.

Quick Reminders to Help You through a Transition

1. Stay open to surprises.
2. Don't "effort" to make a change; just go with the flow.
3. Focus only on what's in front of you, and let that guide you.
4. Don't pretend you know what you are doing.
5. Allow life to happen, and then when something new and exciting enters in, jump on it and take action.

Don't get me wrong. My move wasn't all a happy, romanticized movie moment. It was hell for six weeks, shuttling around before I made it to New York. I was all over the place (emotionally and physically), crashing in too-many friends' homes and hotels until I found an apartment in Chelsea. I threw a rib out from the stress. I was terrified about the move.

I arrived in Manhattan during an April rainstorm. I rushed through crowded, loud, busy downtown streets, fighting fierce wind with my umbrella, soaked and freezing from the downpour. I felt like a complete stranger in a foreign land. As rain pelted my face, my pant legs were soaked to the knees, and cold chills ran through my entire body; I started to think I couldn't handle the change. I wiped tears streaming down my face with the rain, wondering what the hell I was thinking moving to such a big, crazy city. I wanted to immediately fly back home to sunny, laid-back Southern California.

What do we do in these moments, when we're doing everything we can to move forward but feel so close to giving up? What do we do when the going gets tough and we start to question everything? As my painting teacher, Michele, taught, *Don't make resistance the bad guy; listen to it. Resistance is a bell ringing for change.*

I reminded myself, *I asked for this change. It's why I came to New York in the first place.* And even though I felt like I couldn't continue on and wanted to bail out, I knew I wouldn't. This was my bell. And hell yeah, I was going to ring it. Regardless if I was walking against hard wind in the cold rain, I was growing and evolving, and that's all that mattered. I told myself, *It's worth it.* I reminded myself that I was on an adventure, and that's all that mattered even though I had no clue where I was, what I was doing, and who I was.

When a relationship is over, or a job ends, or you're going through a major life change, you may feel a loss of identity. Yet, it's actually in these times when you're freest. You could get scared and sometimes terrified when you can't cling to a definition of who you are, because you think you're dying. In fact, it is a kind of death of how you once perceived yourself. So you could look for ways to grip on to something to feel more secure: a place to feel safe, a refuge from dying. And the way you may do this most is by searching for your identity. You may want to try to attach to something, whether in how you label yourself, or to another person, or seeking answers, or needing to know you are on the right path, or even desiring a spiritual awakening.

But when you hold too tightly, you can feel like you're spinning on a wheel. The more you hold on, the more you can get nauseated and dizzy. If you don't cling to the past, trying to make something that no longer exists make sense, and you don't try to predict and control your future, you're left in the present. It's there in that nonattachment where you achieve your utmost certainty.

Part of being free is being interested in the mystery of all that you aren't. Becoming clearer about who you are not allows you to come closer to your absolute nature.

It's about having a shift in perception and letting go of who you think you should be. Even though you may not have a direct answer when you contemplate who you are not, it's still worthy. It may encourage you to keep being interested in the exploration, to investigate the mystery, to hear your greater call and listen.

When I was turning thirty-four years old and starting to train with Michele to become a teacher, those who wanted to learn her teaching process, if she accepted you, could follow her around the painting studio as she worked with each student individually.

One day, I followed her at a workshop at Esalen in Big Sur. It was hard for me to focus. I was trying to pay attention to her and each individual student, but I was bored. I thought I was hiding it well, but on our lunch break Michele asked to speak to me. She wasn't happy. I had asked to learn from her how to teach her painting process but was instead distracting her by my incessant yawning. I thought I was tired because I didn't sleep well the night before, but when I checked in with myself, I became aware that rather than paying attention to Michele and the student she was working with, I was looking at my own painting, pinned to the wall in the corner. What I was truly wanting was to be painting myself and not following Michele around the studio.

"Why do you want to teach?" Michele asked me.

I had to be honest. "Because I want to feel like I'm not just painting for process, and I've *arrived* somewhere." Painting just for process didn't seem like enough. Becoming one of her coteachers made me feel important; this seemed the next step I should take. But my ego was in my way, wanting recognition. I thought I should make money at it, rather than continuing to pay for workshops. When I humbled myself, I discovered all I really wanted was to just keep painting. It was the fun of the process that made me most happy.

After lunch I returned, relieved, to my painting in the corner. The pressure was off. I didn't *have* to be a teacher. I had permission to paint again without the labels I thought I needed to *become* something, to prove I was *doing* something more. I could just keep on being and painting.

Our mind wants to pigeonhole us in self-identification—the ways we try to narrowly identify ourselves. Nouns can trap us. Nouns such as these: Student. Teacher. Artist. Writer. Lawyer. CEO. Waitress. Parent. . . . The reason why is that when we refer to ourselves as a "noun," we create a solid, fixed sense of self. There's no room for adjustability, fluidity, or infinite possibility. Or, if we aren't making money at what we love to do or haven't received accolades for it, we think it isn't significant or important. Or we do make money at it, and then our sense of self is determined by the jobs we have or how much we've made. This is another way the mind can entrap us; how we lose the innate gift of our freedom.

It's natural to identify ourselves as a "noun." Some of us like having titles because it shows our accomplishments. But is this the only way to perceive ourselves? Are we really only a label?

When we meet someone at a social event, the question usually asked is *What do you do?*

What do you do? leads to an answer in a noun form.

I'd have to say, *I'm a painter and a writer.* But how I reply is always in the verb form: *I paint and write.* Self-identification can lock us into certain, limited roles. It snubs out permission to be *all of who we are.* Without our self-definitions, we think we're nobody. We think we have no distinctiveness. And that's an illusion—far from reality. I mean, let's face it, when we're asked, *What do you do?*, what we're really being asked is *How do you pay your bills?*

When I'm at a social event, I ask, *What do you love?* That leads to a verb.

They might say, *I love windsailing, or helping out at the shelter, or traveling, or playing Mah Jong, or baking.*

Whenever I ask that question, the person's face lights up. Conversation takes off. We're connecting because he or she feels seen. And that's because they're free to be anything. We're not human *doings.* We're human *beings.* What we love is changeable and malleable. At any given time, our passions, sense of self, purpose, and interests change. We're always evolving. We're not limited to just one thing. We get to be everything and nothing. It's not just a party trick I'm getting at here. It's a different point of seeing.

Inner-Freedom Exercise

1. Think about how you identify yourself. Not just your vocations, but who you believe you are, based on your history, degrees, possessions, or family systems; the amount of money you have; your roles; your ideas; or what you have accumulated. Write those down.

2. Has that ensnared you into a certain way of thinking? How might that way of seeing yourself affect your totality?

3. Are you allowing for all of life to work through you? Are you free, living at your highest capacity?

4. What identity/identities might you drop right now to be the most free? Or could you just be *all* of it, free of definition and attachment?

17

Dreams

We all have dreams—dreams we may think could never be. Too often, we put these dreams off, waiting to feel like everything is "right"—the right timing, right environment, right preparation, right education, or right ideas. Because of this, our enthusiasm could wane, our light dim, and our dream fade. However, creativity is calling us over and over, but we keep it in a box like an unopened present, just waiting for our courage.

Why is this voice calling to us to follow a dream, when it knows we have too-many other priorities or can't do it at this time? Because our dreams know better than us. They know more than we do the feeling of bliss we get from doing what we love. They have our back. They know our heart and what it wants to express. They know better than we ever could about what will give us joy and happiness. Creativity wants us to continue to grow into updated versions of ourselves. So, we have opportunities to listen and accomplish our dreams step by step. The more we listen, the more we realize we are being led by something much greater than us, and the more astounded we are by what lives inside us.

Any time I felt uncertain, stuck, or depressed, I came to realize I was not tapping into my dreams. Or I questioned what my dreams were. Or it seemed impossible to achieve. And on really bad days, my inner judge judged my "dreams" as a load of crap. The more we follow our dreams, the more we are on purpose. I thought I had to have the dream all planned out—how I'd do it and what would happen next. But, finally, rather than spend my time wondering if, when, or how it might happen, I came to realize I just needed to start. And a wild world of spontaneity, surprises, and inquiry opened up.

If we take our dreams oh-so-seriously, we might feel like a failure, but mostly we fear success because then we would have to go to another level in ourselves, and it's much safer to remain with what were used to, hiding in our corner. But when there's more room to explore, like on a fun adventure; we can hold our dreams with a lighter hand. It could be fun, instead of having the pressure of some big thing we have to accomplish. Sometimes we deem it as a whim, causing our attention to be only sporadic. We don't allow ourselves the fulfillment of a total experience. Sometimes, the reason for why we're not making time for our dreams on an ongoing basis is because our mind projects out into the future, looking only at the outcome:

- *"There's no way I can create what I want—it's going to take years or I'm too old . . ."*

- *"I've always wanted to achieve this, but I don't know how to go about it . . ."*

- *"I'd love to make my dream come true, but I don't have the time or means to create it . . ."*

Many times when we have so many other things going on in our lives—work, commitments to family and community, daily responsibilities—we don't think we can have our dreams too. Life passes us by until we grow older and die, hopefully not looking back with regret, saying I wish I did *that thing*. Whether it's a bucket list item or an unfulfilled life purpose, or a different career, or a vacation, or any other creative desire, we can always find the way and time to create it. We just have to step out of our own way.

WORKSHEET
Freedom from Inner Blocks

Are you aware of any stories or limiting beliefs that might be in your way of creating your dreams? Is your inner judge's little voice telling you something that isn't true?

1. **Become aware of your limiting beliefs**. Take some time to become aware of the judgments in your head. There may be several. It may be a long list. Awareness is the first step to being free of them. What is your inner judge saying that might be stopping you from creating what you want? What are its excuses? What or whom is it blaming for not being able to have what you want to create? What are the limiting stories your mind is putting on you?

    Write out your answers in your journal. Don't cross out or edit. Allow them to come as a stream-of-consciousness exercise. Just write out the first things that come to mind.

2. **The Ultimate-Lie Statement.** Streamline the paragraph you just wrote into one concise statement. Narrow the judgments down to their root: In one sentence, what is the primary judgment your inner judge is placing on you?

    _____

    _____

3. **Release.** Usually our Ultimate Lie stems from something from our past that's no longer true in the present moment.

    *   Can you see how this ultimate lie is possibly something you picked up from your past that is no longer relevant?

    *   Who taught this lie to you? Where did you pick it up?

    *   Can you drop it?

    *   Is it possible you no longer need to carry it?

Ask yourself:

What if it didn't matter if I felt _____ or not?

Fill in the blank with your Ultimate-Lie Statement. Feel it deeply. Don't just ask the question. Feel it as you ask it, right down to your bones.

- What if it didn't matter or not?
- What if it *really* didn't matter or not?
- How would you react differently?
- How might you get creative about finding another possibility?

What next step would I take anyway?

_____

_____

See yourself, in your mind's eye, as a person who accepted either way: A person who was totally free. Can you now return to manifesting your dreams?

4. **Pinpoint your dreams.** If it were a perfect world, what would "this thing you want to create" look like?

_____

_____

- If concerns about money, irrational beliefs, or other worries weren't in your way, what new interest would you explore?

_____

_____

- If there were no limitations and you could have what you want, what would you do?

_____

_____

- What would you feel like inside while doing this?

_____

_____

- What would you feel like when finished?

_____

_____

Usually, your dream is so thrilled to have your attention that it's just grateful for your willingness to meet it. It's like "*Hi! I've been waiting for you! I'm so happy you're here!*" Even if this process at first feels like drudgery, somehow if you take one step forward, something inside you will wake up. You will feel good about yourself in the simple act of beginning.

Don't put off a dream for another moment. It's calling you for a reason. It knows exactly how it will serve you. It absolutely knows what you need. Do it just because you dig it.

Begin without putting any pressure on yourself. What if:

- It didn't have to be good, or a bestseller, or make a million bucks?
- You didn't have to know anything at first and could learn as you go?
- No one had to know about it for now, and you kept it to yourself?
- You could have this dream; what would be your first step right now?

Don't worry about the outcome when you begin. You can deal with that later. Just begin.

WORKSHEET
Your Dreams in Fruition

1. STEP ONE: Intention

Write your intention for what you want to create. Intention is power that leads to creation. And when we intend to create something, we become magicians who believe in our ability to make magic happen. Whatever we intend can transcend if we stay open and willing to commit to it. Answers to what steps to follow will make themselves apparent later. What you most want *will* come even though you could never know *exactly* what creativity intends for your highest good.

Choose one intention for your Dream in Fruition. You can do as many Dreams-in-Fruition Worksheets as you want for everything you intend to create in your life. But for now, start with one.

For example, "It is my intention to_____."

- Write a novel.
- Have a loving, healthy, long-term relationship.
- Create a new job opportunity.
- Experience better health.
- Have more peace and ease in my life.

Write your intention now:

It is my intention to _____.

2. STEP TWO: Present-Time Creation

Write in present, specific detail what you want to create as if you already have it, as if it were happening right now in your journal. Get specific. Imagining the specifics of the ultimate outcome you want to create may seem like a fantasy at first, but you may discover things you hadn't thought of or seen before, even what you didn't think was realizable. You never know exactly what creativity intends for you. Remaining open to all of life's wonderment, it could create something even better than you believed you could encounter.

Dare to be bold. Don't worry right now if or how it will come to fruition. The point is to dream, because if you can't dream first, you can't ignite your creation.

For example, let's say what you want is to be in a loving relationship. You might write something like:

- I am in a loving relationship with a man/woman I love.

- I am with someone who is caring, respectful, and we share the same values.

- I enjoy sharing daily life with my partner and doing fun things together.

- I am grateful for my beloved's sense of humor.

- I am experiencing passionate chemistry.

Or, an example for having more peace and less stress in your life:

- I am making time for me each day to devote to my own self-care.

- I meditate fifteen minutes a day in the morning when I wake.

- I take long walks in nature three times a week.

- I say no to people who want more of my time than I can give.

Remember to include specific, clear, present detail to infuse your dream with reality. This fertilizes the ground for your vision to grow. All you need is for it to be 52 percent believable. Then you're over halfway there.

Make sure you write in the positive rather than using negatives. For example, "I'm not dating a man who is dishonest," would be instead, "I am dating a man with integrity." Or, "I'm not eating junk food" would be "I eat healthy foods that sustain my body."

3. STEP THREE: Grounding Your Intention

Soon, you're going to read your Dream in Fruition out loud. But before beginning, center yourself in yourself. Take a few moments to ground.

Close your eyes and imagine a cord wider than your hips, tied at the bottom of your sacrum. It can be as wide as you want. Even as big as a football field or even wider. Whatever feels comfortable for you. Have fun with it!

Envision the cord going straight from your sacrum into the center of the Earth and firmly attaching itself to the core.

Rest here for at least a minute or two (or longer), to experience true presence, centering, and grounding.

Then, imagine a big, bright sun's orb in the middle of your chest, permeating your Dream in Fruition with light, love, presence, and attention.

Imagine spreading the light from your chest, filling your whole body from the top of your head to your toes.

Fill the entire room you are in with that light.

Then send it out across the entire city you live in. The state. The country. And end with the light spreading around and beyond the whole world.

Think of this as a very powerful, sacred ritual, drawing to you your manifestations.

Once you are securely grounded and filled with light, spreading that light as far as you can imagine, open your eyes and read your opening intention out loud, and then speak each of your present-time creations, infusing them with certainty and enthusiasm.

4. STEP FOUR: Commit to an Action Step

Whether it's a bucket list item or an unfulfilled life purpose, or a different career, or a vacation, or any other creative desire, you can always find the way and time to create it. You get it started by taking one small step at a time.

If a World Cup soccer player wanted to kick the ball from one goal to the other in one fell kick, the chances of getting his goal is most likely zero percent. But if he dribbled the ball one dribble at a time, he's more likely guaranteed a score. If you just devoted some of your attention and made time, even in small increments, you can reach big dreams, learning and exploring new parts of yourself while having a blast along the way.

Ask yourself:

- What's the easiest thing I could do right now to take action?
- What's the first step I am drawn to take?
- What interests me the most as a place to get started?
- What seems like the most fun?
- What stimulates the most energy inside me?
- What's a realistic, doable, next action that I could start right away?

For example, if it's a relationship you want to create, you might choose your first action step to be joining a social event to meet new people this Saturday night. Or to have more peace and less stress in your life, you might choose your first action step to be to take a forty-five-minute beginners' yoga class this Sunday.

When writing your action step, include the time or date you are committing to do it. The earlier the better; in fact, you might as well start now. Make it something small. Keep it easy, something manageable, something that doesn't take a lot of time or that's a big deal. You don't have to tell anyone about this. Sometimes keeping this to yourself for a little while helps to protect the baby seed as it grows into a sapling.

Write your first action step in the blank and include the time and date:

My first action step is _____, and I will complete this by _____ on _____.

5. STEP FIVE: Continue

After completing this action step, create a new one. Commit to another time and a date. Keep it small. Keep it easy. Make it doable. Do one action step at the very least once a week. Don't take on too much. But don't do too little. Set it up so that it's realistic to continue.

Continue on like this: one action step at a time to reach your dreams.

Once a week for the next month, read your Dream in Fruition out loud. Invoke the sun in the middle of your chest as you read. Infuse it with light, and in your mind's eye, spread the sunshine out. Keep infusing your dream with loving, light-filled energy as you take each small action step, and watch what you want to create miraculously unfold.

It really works. Here's to the sun's light and making all your dreams come true.

Love

Within only a month of living in New York, I soon became acclimated and excited about enjoying all of what the city offered. I took 5 Rhythms classes every Tuesday night at the top of the Joffrey Ballet on 6th Avenue, dancing barefoot to loud beats and letting my wild woman come through. When I needed to catch my breath, I'd look out of the picturesque windows down to the line of yellow cabs, in awe of living in such a fun, crazy city. Just like my intuition told me it would, New York energized me. I took long walks on sidewalks full of eclectic people, window shopped, and strolled through urban parks. I sat at restaurant bars by myself and struck up friendly conversations—and even made new friends. I attended gallery shows, exhibitions, Broadway shows, and off-Broadway theater and went to literary salons in writers' homes to listen to them read just like I was in a Woody Allen movie. I started a new business helping people to be creatively free. Many of my friends from Los Angeles came to stay with me as we explored the city together. I rarely, if ever, felt lonely.

I started dating using dating apps and met a lot of interesting men. Something had changed in me. I wasn't grasping for a relationship; I wasn't grasping for anything. I didn't need anyone like I had in the past to fill my empty spaces. I was standing on my own two feet for the first without my mother and father, without a man to protect me, or a dog to take care of. I was free and simply enjoying the process of connecting with different kinds of people. It seemed that the losses had now strengthened me, and I'd developed a previously unknown self-confidence.

Five years after my life fell apart, I swiped right on a man's picture. His profile read, "Part artist. Part scientist. Part magician. I've performed my work for Kings and Queens, in the Olympics, and with Cirque du Soleil and on Broadway every day. Looking for something real."

We texted, and I told him I was forty-seven and an artist too. He wanted to meet me the following week when he got back from doing a performance in Marrakesh. For reasons that I could not understand, I had a feeling about Dan before we even met.

He invited me to a quaint and special tapas restaurant a few blocks from my apartment. It was December 15, 2016, the first night of that winter season when temperatures dropped below freezing.

I gave the maître d' my black faux-fur winter coat and approached Dan, who was sitting in the corner at the bar. I sat on the stool next to him, and a few moments later as I adjusted in my seat, he reached between my legs to grab the leg of the stool and pulled it right up to him, looking straight into me.

Sitting there with his knee pressed against my thigh, I just knew. I could tell he knew too.

We ate razor clams and drank red wine. He showed me pictures of his son, Sam, who was five years old, and his recent art installation in the center of the world's fair in Astana, Kazakhstan.

"We're cut from the same cloth," he said after hours of conversation.

Dan then came over every subsequent day. A week later, he said he wanted to take me Brooklyn to show me his art studio. As we drove in his car, he squeezed my thigh hard.

The Avett Brothers' song "I and Love and You" was playing on his stereo. I watched the traffic in front of me and the bicyclists whiz between cars. I looked up at the tall buildings on either side. The day was chilly and gray, and the few trees in the city streets were barren.

We crossed over the Williamsburg Bridge, and I looked behind to the island of Manhattan, in awe of its magnificent skyline and overcome by where I'd landed.

I turned my head to look out my window so that he couldn't see me sobbing, but there was no way I could hide. I knew in that moment that my new life had begun. I had reached my destination.

"Why are you crying?" he asked me.

"I can't believe it's all over," I told him. "The grief, the pain, the loss, the difficult years—it's now all in the past."

Dan squeezed my thigh tighter as he hid the tears welling up in his eyes too.

He showed me his art studio, a black box in the center of Williamsburg filled with collected years of sculptures made of every medium possible: fabric, stone, wood, glass, rubber, plastic, and more. A wooden staircase he built by hand led to a loft that was his office. When he was upstairs, without wanting him to see, I picked up a feather off the concrete floor and a small handful of glitter and put it in my jacket's pocket to remember the moment I first went to his gallery, which seemed auspicious to me, because I had this feeling I would be involved with his art for the rest of our lives. He then came down and took my arm to walk me a few blocks to his favorite neighborhood Middle Eastern restaurant.

Seated at a table for two in the corner, waiting for our food, Dan surprised me.

"I've been thinking about how important it is that you meet your biological mother."

"What?" I said.

"Yes, otherwise it might be something you'll regret. If you want, I'd be happy to go with you."

"You would do that with me?"

"Yes, of course I would."

It had always been a dream of mine that one day I would meet my soul mate and he would go with me to meet Renee. Rather than go and see her in a childish place of neediness, I wanted to be grounded, my own person, settled in my own life and at home in a relationship.

"Regardless if the connection is good or bad, you'll know it's something you won't regret not doing. C'mon," he said as he held my hand. "Let's go."

"I'm open to that possibility." It was curious I said this, but it rang true. I was no longer pushing love away, no longer seeing my life through the wound of being adopted. Because I had arrived at a place of having a deep relationship with myself, I no longer needed the love and validation from a mother or father, nor from a man for that matter. In that instant, my perspective changed.

"We are family," Dan said. "My fervent hope is that with Sam and I, you will have a sense of family you've always wanted. Let's close this chapter with your bio-mom and move on."

That evening I called Renee. It had been years since we last spoke. She was happy to hear from me.

"I have a new boyfriend," I told her. "And we were talking. He'd like to come with me to meet you."

"Are you ready?" she asked me.

"Yes, I think I am."

"You know, I never wanted you to feel pressured. It's been important to me that you know you can have your space. I've been giving this to you for the past ten years."

"Thank you, Renee," I told her. "What do you think about meeting on our birthday?" I blurted this out, not thinking if it was a good idea or not, but September 2 was many months away, and I knew that would give me time to prepare. Of course I'd never forgotten her telling me in our very first phone call that we had the same birthday.

"I think that would be lovely," she said. "Why don't I come to New York?" Renee asked me. I liked that she was willing to come to me.

I acknowledged Renee's courage and strength to give me the space that I had needed. I also inwardly acknowledged the courage I now had to meet her. It was my life to lead. I felt empowered.

On September 2, 2017, the buzzer rang at 10:20 a.m., and I watched the elevator panel in my apartment numbers go from one to eleven.

"Hi Renee," I said welcoming her as the elevator doors opened. "Here we are."

"Well, here we are," she said.

We both laughed uncomfortably as we stood in front of each other.

"You're so beautiful," she said.

I leaned down to give her a light hug. "Thank you! You are, too."

"Are you nervous?" Renee asked me as I laughed more nervously.

"Well, of course I am. I didn't sleep all night."

I immediately noticed our same eyes and mouth. "Do we have the same nose?" I asked her.

"Your nose is pointier."

"Would you like some tea?"

"Sure," she said.

She settled onto the bar stool at the kitchen counter, while I filled mugs with water and put them in the microwave with herbal tea bags. She sat her purse on the kitchen counter; I was immediately taken aback by it. I carried the exact same one.

"I'm glad we're doing this," she said with her arms resting on the counter and her hands folded together.

"Me, too. It seems easy," I concurred.

"You've grown so much since our first conversation," Renee told me in a motherly way.

I offered that we go to lunch at a café around the corner from my apartment. I went to get my purse from my desk.

"You're not going to believe this, Renee," I said, walking to my desk. "But we have the same purse." I picked it up and showed her.

"Oh my God!" she exclaimed. "We have to take a picture."

We gathered next to each other and aimed her phone upward to try to photograph the bags over both our crossed shoulders, while keeping our faces in the lens, proof we were alike in many ways. We both delighted in our similarities.

While we walked to lunch she took my hand, and I let her. I thought to myself, love could be shared in many ways. And although she was not my mother, I cared.

When we said our goodbyes, I felt complete. Our meeting was simple and sweet.

A little more than a month later, at ten on a glorious Paris sun-shining fall brisk morning, Dan led me tightly around my waist to the Pont des Arts across the Seine. Standing at the center, near the edge, with the Ile de la Cité and Notre Dame in the near distance, Dan got on one knee and proposed with the ring we had chosen at a nearby boutique. Then, we sealed our love with a padlock with a painted heart on it that Dan got, locking it onto the bridge. We sat on a bench as he popped a bottle of champagne, and the cork flew several yards, almost hitting a pedestrian. We sat there for an hour talking like we always did about our future creative projects, and we were excited about the house we found and loved and were about to purchase in Westchester to have shared custody of Sam, who was about to turn six.

Our new home rested a short distance from the Hudson River. We moved in December a year after we first met; a spruce tree higher than our house was centered proudly in front of us. A lone wooden fence marked our property line in the six-inch-deep snow, and the sun's bright orange orb lowered itself every evening behind the gleaming water. The green tips of the pines were dusted with white. The driveway hadn't been shoveled since a blizzard blew through, and it was a frigid five degrees.

Dan made a fire in the living room with small kindling and thin cut logs, cut with a hatchet by Sam, wearing ski pants, a winter coat, and heavy gloves. Sam took pride that his father taught him to use heavy tools responsibly. He was strong, and resilient, courageous, tender, smart, and sensitive. I loved his free, expressive, creative nature.

In the kitchen I was roasting broccoli, the only vegetable Sam would eat, gnawing the burly heads off and leaving the stems to the side. We would grill steak and bake some potatoes cut into slivers like fries.

"Lynn?" Sam asked me in the kitchen, in his endearing way full of love.

"Yes?" I replied.

"When you and Dad get married and you're my stepmom, do I call you Mom?"

"No, you will call me Lynn. Just like you call me now."

"But it's easier to call you Mom."

"You'll call me Lynn," I said kindly, full of love.

"But I want to call you Mom."

I knew Sam was trying to understand this change. He had a very close relationship, full of love, with his mother, who lived ten minutes away from us. I understood the confusion: Who is my mother? And how can I love them both? And am I loved by the two the same?

I respected this fact. I was not his mother, and it wasn't right for him to call me Mom. I understood how we could love one another like a mother and son without biological connections.

Sam sweetly put his arms out to me and curled into my side, nestling his head.

I was astonished I had a child in my life. One that I never thought I would have. I realized I didn't want to be a mother based on mistruths: I would never be good enough. I was not perfect. But life had another plan. And the plan was to love those who were put in front of me, in every stage of life, no matter where I was or where I ended up, because they were each perfectly chosen for me. Even though he was not my son, I loved him beyond belief. My heart opened even wider.

Dan walked into the kitchen and saw Sam leaning against me. Dan tried to hide his tears as he wiped his eyes with manly, somewhat gnarled tool-injured fingers, badges of honor of his years of work as a sculptor. He picked Sam up over his shoulder as he kicked wildly and laughed. I stood at the sink in front of the picture window, looking out at our abundance of trees and thinking about my mother. Oh, how she would have loved seeing the changes I had made in becoming a whole person, and how thrilled she would be for me. And I thought about my father. How good he would feel that I was now really being taken care of. I thought to myself, "Yes, love takes a big container, a huge opening up. Without needing a title. Without being defined. Even without anything having to making any sense. Surrendering to all that life offers, we dive into love." And I asked myself, "How big can I be? How much larger can my love be without a boundary?"

As I heard Dan and Sam playing together in the background, happy tears fell off my cheeks into the sink.

"Lynn?" Sam called out to me.

"Yes, love." I said, grabbing a paper towel and wiping fast.

"I'm hungry."

"Let's eat!" I said. And for my adoptive mother I said, "Help me put the plates on the table."

"Okay!" he said and came and grabbed the stack of dishes from my hand.

I put the food out. Dan cracked a joke. Sam made a funny face and giggled. And the story of my past was over, like that. My new life beamed down on me proudly and with overabounding joy and happiness.

Conclusion

> *Life is a play that does not allow testing. So, sing, cry, dance, laugh, and live intensely, before the curtain closes and the piece ends with no applause.*

—Charlie Chaplin

Review Worksheet

To create the life you really want, remember these important life-changing questions:

- What gives you "juice"?
- Where is the energy calling you?
- What if you gave yourself full permission to engage?

Going toward what gives you energy and meeting it fully is the first step to creating profound change.

- What if you took a risk?
- What if you dove off the high board?
- What if you didn't second-guess yourself?
- What if you were spontaneous?
- What if whatever you did you couldn't fail?

Dare to fail brilliantly. Taking risks jolts us into the new and creates immediate change.

What would happen if:

- You followed your gut?
- You listened to your intuition rather than your mind's judgment?
- You thought later and created now?

Creating what we want doesn't happen in the future; it happens today.

How about:

- Exploring?
- Using everything as a learning opportunity?
- Daring to discover?
- Letting go of what you think you know?

Love the unknown and let the mystery unfold.

And what about:

- Focusing on play and fun?
- Not worrying about what people think or comparing yourself?
- Dropping the stories collected over the years and invoking the essence of your child self?
- Creating just for the sake of creating and let the rest organically unfold?
- Letting loose and getting messy?
- Going a little crazy?
- Doing something you never thought you would do?
- Unleashing?
- Holding a loving, safe container for yourself as you expressed what is innately inside of you?

- Giving yourself permission to be it all: the good, the bad and the ugly?
- Accepting all of what was in front of you?

Welcome the places that may make you feel uncomfortable or fearful, and use these situations as catalysts for change. Welcoming what makes you uncomfortable will open you up to a new way of being. Let your inner adventurer guide you to the places you may not otherwise dare to go to be free.

How about:

- Being fully present.
- Connecting to your heart center.
- Not holding onto the past or reaching for the future.
- Not worrying about what could happen.
- Stayed determined.
- Not giving up.
- Beginning by doing the easiest thing you could do.
- Taking it one step at a time.
- Showing up when you said you would.

It's in the follow through where creativity blooms. Gently approaching what we want to create each and every day is how we ultimately create change.

And how about:

- Allowing space and time.
- Not forcing the current or need everything to flow the way you want it.
- Accepting life's natural timing.
- Making the result not nearly as important as the experience.
- Using everything as an opportunity to discover.
- Not needing to know who you are.
- Being free to be, express, and create however you're called.

- Letting your freedom be the greatest source of your happiness.
- Not searching for answers, or meaning, or trying to make sense of it all.
- Listening to Love instead of fear.

We are innately creative beings whether we realize it or not. Change is a creative process. To become anew, begin with meeting your wildest dreams. Let's travel together through this amazing thing called life. I'll meet you there, happily.

Acknowledgments

Thank you to my teachers over the last twenty years who gave me gems of wisdom that were priceless. Without you I wouldn't have learned these creative life tools that changed me and now give me such joy to teach.

And for those whom I was in relationship with in the past, who were my ultimate teachers, thank you for our time together; it was because of you that I could grow into the woman I was meant to be.

For Dinah Roseberry, my editor extraordinaire, who continues to create opportunities for me and for Schiffer Publishing for publishing my visions as I dreamed they could be.

To those who touched these pages with their talented creative nuances: Daniel Wurtzel—the love of my life, Royal Young, Paige McGreevy, Nikki Groom, Marisa Goudy, Sue Shapiro, Lisa Sarkissian, and many others who took the time to support me.

To those who have read my blogs for the past many years, I couldn't have done this without you. In fact, it was because of YOU that this book came into fruition. Thank you for continually reading and giving me more purpose in my life. I am eternally grateful for you.

To Marty and Russ, Gail, Hannah, Rachel, and Jamie—our loss brought us closer together. I love you so dearly.

Last, to Mom and Dad, thank you for your permission to be all that I have ever wanted to be without question. As you did every morning when you awoke, counting your many blessings with each other while having coffee, I too awake counting my many blessings for you. You may no longer be with me, but I know you are beaming down proudly. And damn, that feels good.

Your Muse Notes

Faced with a string of crippling losses, **Lynn Newman**
found herself with no choice but to trust her inner muse
to light the way. The experience taught her that the
greatest art we can create is a truly lived life.
Lynn is a creativity expert who has a bachelor of fine arts
and a master's in counseling psychology.
She's worked as a therapist and a spiritual teacher.
An author and a painter, she is the creator of
The Game of You and *The Game of Insight*.
She lives in New York. To find out more, go to:

LynnNewman.com
FB: LynnZavaroNewman
IG: LynnNewman101
YouTube: Lynn Newman